One of the best, most accurate, yet loving, critiques of the Charismatic movement to date. It is written by one who is unashamedly a Charismatic but sees faults and grave dangers that some are afraid to confront. Dr. Michael Brown hits the nail on the head. This is must-reading for anyone who values the Charismatic movement and its future.

—R. T. Kendall, DPhil
Author; Former Minister, Westminster Chapel

I find myself saying, "Amen! Amen! Amen!" This book is so needed right now! People eager for revelation yet not grounded in Scripture make easy targets for charlatans to exploit them and unsound teachings to move them. May God awaken His church.

—Craig S. Keener, PhD
F. M. and Ada Thompson Professor of Biblical Studies,
Asbury Theological Seminary

Dr. Michael Brown offers a compelling, careful, and honest critique of the current Pentecostal-Charismatic movement. Michael astutely observes that while many wonderful things are taking place by and in the Spirit, there are also aberrations and abuses that require accountability and rectification. My prayer is that we all take heed and listen to what he wisely offers based on his observations and that we too once again learn how to more accurately and carefully discern what the Spirit is saying to the churches.

—Mark J. Chironna, PhD
Founding Pastor, Church on the Living Edge;
Mark Chironna Ministries
Orlando, Florida

The Pentecostal-Charismatic ... amazingly vibrant. It is by far t ... lobal phenomenon in the history of Christianity. It should not be surprising that something so dynamic would come with its share of challenges and issues. But for too long many of the abuses and errors in our midst have gone unaddressed. We are overdue for a much-needed correction. While some would love to throw out the baby with the bathwater, many of us see the precious work that God is doing and are willing to contend for it. This is what the apostle Paul did in Corinth, and it is what is needed in the Charismatic movement today.

In *Playing With Holy Fire* Dr. Michael Brown addresses many of these challenges, not as an outside cynic throwing stones but as a concerned elder and father who has been a part of the movement for well over forty years. In the past Dr. Brown has often stood as a staunch defender of Charismatics and of the moving of the Spirit. But now he is bringing a much-needed word of correction to his own beloved spiritual family. He has managed to strike a nearly impossible balance, being not only brutally honest but also gracious and life-giving. *Playing With Holy Fire* is convicting but also constructive. Dr. Brown has earned the right to speak to our community, and now his message needs to be heard more than ever. It's time for us to put our house in order and prepare for God to move as never before.

—Evangelist Daniel Kolenda
President and CEO, Christ for All Nations

Dr. Michael Brown is a prolific writer, dynamic speaker, and brilliant academic. His books and teachings have been a personal source of encouragement, inspiration, and guidance for me over the past twenty-one years. *Playing With Holy Fire* is another clarion call to leaders and Christians around the world, a sobering warning to the body of Christ. May the holy fire of God set you ablaze as you read this book.

—Ward Simpson
President and CEO, GOD TV

Some people have passion, and that is good. Some people have intellect, and that is good. Few people seem to have large doses of both. But there is an exception. Dr. Michael Brown has both! He is one of the most respected voices in the church today, especially in the Charismatic movement, combining a heart for revival with sound scholarship and prophetic insight. God's people need to listen carefully when he speaks.

—Jim Garlow, PhD
Senior Pastor, Skyline Church
San Diego, California

Dr. Michael Brown is one of the most important prophetic voices in the church today! In *Playing With Holy Fire* he calls out the dysfunction and challenges us in the Charismatic community to raise the standard—big time. We must do so if we are going to see the Lamb receive the reward of His suffering—which is the nations. As one who is constantly exposed to the inner workings of the Charismatic community—and a very proud part of it—I recognize there is much purity mixed with grievous error.

This book will give you an informed, balanced, insider's look at some of the dangers that attempt to distort the Charismatic movement. Dr. Brown is not a critic on the outside looking in; he is someone who has been a part of the Spirit-empowered community ever since he came to faith in the Messiah. He doesn't just call out issues; he calls forth biblical solutions, not attempting to "quench the Spirit" but to create a culture where the church can experience the Spirit in a greater measure because our experience is in complete agreement with what's outlined in Scripture.

—Larry Sparks, MDiv

Publisher, Destiny Image

Author, *Breakthrough Faith*;

coauthor, *The Fire That Never Sleeps*

Dr. Michael Brown is a friend of mine who is never afraid of tackling controversial issues head-on. His prophetic call to the body of Christ, coupled with his high-level scholarship, enables him to speak and write as few can in the church today. In this book Dr. Brown brings a course correction and deals with some extremes found in the Charismatic movement. Both Evangelical and Charismatic leaders can benefit from this important work!

—Dr. Joseph Mattera

National Convener, US Coalition of Apostolic Leaders

I've known Dr. Brown for over three decades and have respected his unwavering, tenacious, and courageous commitment to God and His Word. Motivated by a passion for God and compassion for people, even those who may adamantly disagree with him, Dr. Brown continues to seek to reflect Christ in the love of the truth and demonstrated with grace.

I trust that those who read through this book with humility, honesty, and personal review will be encouraged to think deeper and to draw closer to the Lord. This book challenges the church to consider where we have allowed the enemy in our camp, even if he appears as an angel of light, and denounces the deception that seeks to misguide many believers. This book not only aides us but provokes and challenges us to get back to being lovers of biblical truth, shedding light on areas where we may have drifted from our moorings and helping us to get back to "high noon" with the

Father of Lights, where there is no shadow turning. Personally I found the book to be heart provoking, yet refreshing.

We must keep our eyes fixed on Jesus, our plumb line of truth and righteousness, healing and hope.

—Doug Stringer
President, Turning Point Ministries International and
Somebody Cares America

I have known Dr. Brown for many years and have found him to be a vigilant watchman for truth. This book is a must-read for all Christians who desire to honor our spiritual heritage while preparing for a tremendous future harvest. The passion, power, and purity of former days must be passed on with biblical clarity as we pass on practical and best practices. Dr. Brown's book does this and more.

I read the book from cover to cover in one sitting. It affirmed many of my spiritual values and gave me hope for the future. I commend Dr. Brown for writing this page-turner that will instruct young and old, black and white, male and female during this season of division, dissension, and doctrinal imbalance.

—Bishop Harry Jackson
Founder and Chairman, High Impact Leadership Coalition
Senior Pastor, Hope Christian Church
Beltsville, Maryland

Playing With *Holy* Fire

Playing With *Holy* Fire

MICHAEL L. BROWN, PhD

CHARISMA HOUSE

Most Charisma House Book Group products are available at special quantity discounts for bulk purchase for sales promotions, premiums, fund-raising, and educational needs. For details, write Charisma House Book Group, 600 Rinehart Road, Lake Mary, Florida 32746, or telephone (407) 333-0600.

Playing With Holy Fire by Michael L. Brown, PhD
Published by Charisma House
Charisma Media/Charisma House Book Group
600 Rinehart Road
Lake Mary, Florida 32746
www.charismahouse.com

Cover design by Justin Evans

Visit the author's website at askdrbrown.org.

Library of Congress Cataloging-in-Publication Data:
An application to register this book for cataloging has been submitted to the Library of Congress.
International Standard Book Number: 978-1-62999-498-7
E-book ISBN: 978-1-62999-499-4

18 19 20 21 22 — 9 8 7 6 5 4 3 2 1
Printed in the United States of America

CONTENTS

Preface

I have written this book as an insider, as someone who was saved in a Pentecostal church in 1971 and someone who has spent the better part of the last forty-six years ministering in "Spirit-filled" circles. As painful as some of this book may be for you to read, and was for me to write, I believe it is a necessary pain, similar to the pain inflicted by a surgeon who successfully removes cancer from a patient. It is a life-giving pain, a liberating pain, a purifying pain. It is the pain of love.

And I have written this book as a wholehearted, unapologetic, Pentecostal-Charismatic believer rather than as a hardened cynic. I love the work of the Spirit, and around the world I have witnessed the Spirit's wondrous acts, all in the name of Jesus and for the good of a hurting world. I would have to turn off my brain to deny what I have seen with my own eyes and heard with my own ears. More importantly, I would have to lose my spiritual and academic integrity to ignore the overwhelming scriptural evidence that the supernatural gifts of the Spirit remain active to this day.

At the same time, I would have to live in a small cave to deny that there are rampant serious abuses taking place in the name of the Spirit on a regular basis. Worse still, very little is being done to correct these abuses, which make a mockery of the movement I so deeply love, giving our critics a field day.

That being said, I have not written this book in response to our critics, however sincere they may be. I realize that as long as I remain a fully committed Pentecostal-Charismatic, I will never appease them. And even though some of these critics are godly followers of Jesus, I'm not writing this book to win their approval, as if I needed to demonstrate that I'm better than those other really flaky or even corrupt Pentecostals and Charismatics.

To the contrary, I've written this book *despite* the critics, since: 1) what I write will add fuel to their fire; 2) many of them will misunderstand my motives in writing (again, thinking I'm responding to their criticisms or feeling the need to defend my beliefs or prove my "orthodoxy"); and 3) I couldn't care less what the critics have to say if their criticisms are false or biased or unbiblical. Instead, I'm writing for one reason alone: I'm burdened about the state of the Pentecostal-Charismatic church worldwide, and I'm concerned about the name and reputation of Jesus.

On the positive side—and it is incredibly positive—the Holy Spirit is moving mightily around the world to the point that over the last hundred-plus years we have witnessed the greatest harvest of souls in history. And this harvest is directly and undeniably related to the Pentecostal-Charismatic outpouring, dating back to the Azusa Street Revival and its precursors. Whole continents, such as Africa, have been rocked by this spiritual outpouring, and the fruit continues to grow exponentially worldwide.

On the negative side, this outpouring has been mixed with immaturity, gullibility, carnality, sensationalism, merchandising, corruption, and doctrinal error, much of it stemming from the rapid growth of this supernatural movement. In many ways today's situation is an exaggerated picture of what happened in Corinth (or, I should say, a much larger example of what happened in Corinth), where the Holy Spirit was moving mightily, yet there was immaturity, carnality, immorality, doctrinal error, and fascination with superstar leaders.

In writing to the Corinthians, Paul commended them, saying, "You do not lack any spiritual gift as you eagerly wait for our Lord

Jesus Christ to be revealed" (1 Cor. 1:7, NIV). At the same time, his letters were filled with correction, some of it very strong. Yet he never denied that the Spirit was at work in their midst (as many critics do today). Instead, he brought correction and direction amid the Spirit's outpouring, giving the believers instructions on the proper use of these sacred gifts of God.

That is what I intend to do in the pages that follow, not as God's policeman or as some kind of Pentecostal pope. Rather, as an elder in the faith who wholeheartedly believes in the outpouring of the Spirit today, I make an appeal to my Pentecostal-Charismatic brothers and sisters, especially to my fellow leaders: it's time for us to set our house in order.

I truly believe the Spirit's work will intensify in the coming years, and we will see an even greater harvest worldwide. All the more reason, then, for us to get our spiritual houses in order so that when the heavy rain comes pouring down, it will refresh us rather than destroy us.

Throughout the book I cite specific examples of errors and abuses I have witnessed myself or heard from reliable sources. However, I have chosen not to name names, despite some critics urging me to do so. To be sure, I recognize that there *are* times to name names, and in some of my other books I do so in detail, with quotes and sources. In this case I chose not to for several reasons.

First, some of those I reference may have changed over the years, and I wouldn't want to blemish them if they have truly repented. Second, some of the leaders I speak of are godly people with blind spots, yet the moment I point out a blind spot, others will reject their whole ministry, since we tend to throw the baby out with the bathwater.

Third, in contrast with my book *Hyper-Grace*, in many cases I can't offer specific, documented quotes as much as reliable stories and anecdotes. Plus, I can't reach out first to every person I reference in the book, as I sought to do, for the most part, when writing *Hyper-Grace*.[1] Fourth, some things take place in countries such as those in Africa that are outside my direct view. In those cases, even when I have reliable eyewitness reports, I don't believe it's right to name a name based on that alone.

Fifth, I'm also addressing general tendencies, so by citing an example, I'm addressing the larger issue. Sixth, in not naming names, I'm following a New Testament precedent, since the writers sometimes named names (e.g., 1 Tim. 1:19–20; 2 Tim. 4:14; 3 John 1:9) and sometimes did not (e.g., 2 Pet. 2:1–22; 2 Cor. 11:13–15). In the latter case, we can assume that by the writers' describing the error or abuse, the people would then know who was being described. The same holds true here.

Either way, whether or not names are named, if the shoe fits, wear it. If you're a leader and you're convicted by the words in this book, then humble yourself before God in repentance, and He will give you grace. If you're a believer and you're convicted by these words, the Lord will help you grow and mature as you lean hard on Him. And to leaders whose sin is failing to address the error of others, may the Lord give you courage and resolve to speak the truth in love, regardless of cost and consequence. You cannot afford *not* to speak.

Finally, I need to explain why I often refer to some leaders as prophets or apostles even if I feel they're in error. First, there are true apostles and prophets who are in error in one particular area of their ministry. That alone doesn't disqualify them from being described as apostles or prophets any more than it disqualifies a pastor who is in error in one particular area of his ministry from being described as a pastor. Second, there's sometimes a fine line between "so-called apostle" and "false apostle," or between a genuine apostle acting wrongly and a "so-called apostle." Rather than try to split hairs, I generally used the terms these leaders use to describe themselves. Let the burden of proof be on them.

Third, throughout the Old Testament false prophets are often referred to as prophets (e.g., Jer. 23:9–40; 27:9, 14; 28:5, 10, 12, 15, 17). They looked like prophets and ministered as prophets, but they were not speaking for the Lord. In the same way, if someone claims to be an apostle or prophet today, I generally refer to that person in that way, which only heightens the depth of their error and the greatness of their accountability to God. Fourth, in my understanding, false prophets and false teachers are hell-bound deceivers who lead others to hell. (See Matthew 7:15–20; 2 Corinthians 11:13–15; 2 Peter 2:1–22.) So if a true believer falsely claims to be a prophet or prophesies falsely, I will address the person's error, but I will not call that person a "false prophet." Others use these terms differently, but unless I feel quite sure the person in question is a complete heretic or charlatan, I won't brand him or her a false prophet, false teacher, or false apostle.

Having said all this, let me repeat: God is doing unprecedented, glorious things in the Charismatic church worldwide, and I believe He wants to do far greater things in the days ahead. That's why it's essential that we get our house in order today. Join with me now in praying, "Speak, Lord! Your servant is listening."

Foreword

Dr. Michael Brown's book *Playing With Holy Fire* issues a call to the Pentecostal and Charismatic camps to self-police their ranks, as he points out many problems within the two groups. Dr. Brown is faithful to acknowledge that these problems also occur among the Evangelical wing of the church, and I would add that they are present within the liberal wing as well. However, what piqued my interest was when Dr. Brown asked whether the Pentecostal and Charismatic camps are more vulnerable to certain sins, mistakes, and foolish—if not at times outlandish—views.

In the first two chapters Dr. Brown deals with the Pentecostal-Charismatic movement's phenomenal success in reaching the lost and the tremendous numerical growth that has brought, as well as why there is more gullibility among Pentecostals and Charismatics than among Evangelicals. Dr. Brown brings constructive criticism of ministries that are too focused on finances and leaders who live and behave more like movie or sports superstars than servants. He also draws attention to the abusive, manipulative, controlling leaders and pastors; the movement's failure to discern, judge, and weigh prophetic words, which has led to abuse, foolishness, and unbiblical practices; and sexual immorality. I would think sexual immorality among Pentecostals and Charismatics wouldn't be worse than it is among Evangelical or theologically liberal leaders. But regardless, too much occurs, and it has caused some to turn away from the church.

Dr. Brown also shines a spotlight on the extremes of the

prosperity gospel. Although it is not the gospel most Pentecostal and Charismatic churches preach, those who do teach this gospel have created a problem for the rest of the church. He goes on to address novel, unbiblical doctrinal positions based upon poor exegesis and that sometimes veer into heresy, and supernatural experiences that seem to fall short of the biblical record and differ strongly from the kinds of experiences written about in past and contemporary church history—the kinds of encounters that leave the people undone and unable to put into words what they saw or experienced.

I agree with the emphasis Dr. Brown gives every chapter of this book. It is an appeal to the Pentecostal-Charismatic community to judge ourselves lest we receive a much more severe judgment from others. It is the truth spoken in love.

Yet despite all the shortcomings of some Pentecostal and Charismatic churches, Dr. Brown ends the book by explaining why he cannot be convinced of the cessationist position of many critics of the Pentecostal-Charismatic movement. He gave two primary reasons. First and most important is that the Bible strongly refutes the view that some of the gifts of the Holy Spirit have ceased and are no longer for the church today. The Bible clearly states otherwise. Second, his experience with the gifts of the Spirit and the fruit they bring to advance the kingdom of God and grow the church makes it impossible to deny the reality of the Pentecostal-Charismatic experience. I would add this is also true of the Third Wave Evangelical continuationist position.

I give a hearty amen to each of the major points in *Playing With Holy Fire* and an amen to Dr. Brown's commitment to the biblical position of continuationism with its belief that all the gifts of the Spirit are still available and active in the church today. Abuse should not lead to neglect but to correction.

—Randy Clark, DMin
Overseer, The Apostolic Network of Global Awakening
Founder, Global Awakening
Author, *There Is More!* and *Power to Heal*

Chapter One
The Spirit Is Moving Mightily!

On July 16, 1999, *Life Magazine* produced an illustrated book titled *The Life Millennium: The 100 Most Important Events and People of the Past 1,000 Years*, edited by Robert Friedman.[1] Producing such a work required a team of hundreds of scholars and experts, some specializing in history, others in the arts, and still others in technology. How difficult it must have been to narrow down the one hundred most important events and people of the past one thousand years! We're talking about things such as Columbus' arrival in America, the first man to step on the moon, the bombing of Hiroshima and Nagasaki, and the invention of electricity—all of them momentous events of massive scope and impact.

That's why it is all the more remarkable that number sixty-eight on the list was the Azusa Street Revival, which began in 1906 and from which the modern Pentecostal movement spread across the globe. Yes, Azusa Street! This event—a spiritual outpouring, not a war or a technological breakthrough or the birth or death of a world leader—made it on a list of the top one hundred events and people of the last thousand years. This is highly significant.

Who would have believed that these relatively small meetings at the Azusa Street Mission, normally attended by just a few hundred people at a time, would have such a global effect, ultimately impacting upwards of one billion people![2] Who would have imagined that these Holy Ghost gospel services, conducted in a former stable described at the time as a "tumble-down shack,"[3] would be ranked ahead of things such as the discovery of anatomy through dissection (number sixty-nine) and the birth of the modern environmental movement (number seventy) in world significance! Who would have conceived that this revival movement, led by an uneducated black preacher who was blind in one eye and the son of freed slaves, would literally shake the world!

The entry in the *Life* book reads:

> 1906. PENTECOSTALISM. The flame of Pentecostalism was first lit when Charles Fox Parham declared in 1901 that speaking in tongues was a sign of baptism in the Holy Spirit. It might have sputtered if not for William Joseph Seymour, a black preacher who listened through an open door to Parham at his Houston Bible school. Soon Seymour set out for Los Angeles, where his own baptism in the Spirit in 1906 brought him an enthusiastic following. He founded a mission in an abandoned church on Azusa Street, and within two years his multicultural ministry had sent missionaries to 25 countries.... Today [1998] about half a billion people call themselves Pentecostal or Charismatic, and Pentecostals outnumber Anglicans, Baptists, Lutherans, and Presbyterians combined.[4]

Back in 1906, in that ramshackle building with that little group of believers, who would have imagined all this!

The importance of the modern Pentecostal movement also caught the attention of Oxford University Press, one of the most respected academic publishing houses in the world. That's why the second volume in its major new series, Oxford Studies in World Christianity, is called *To the Ends of the Earth: Pentecostalism and the Transformation of World Christianity.*[5] This is something that cannot be ignored.

According to series editor Lamin Sanneh:

> In 1950, some 80 percent of the world's Christians lived in the northern hemisphere in Europe and North America. By 2005 the vast majority of Christians lived in the southern hemisphere in Asia, Africa, and Latin America. In 1900 at the outset of colonial rule there were just under 9 million Christians in Africa, of whom the vast majority were Ethiopian Orthodox or Coptic. In 1960 at the end of the colonial period the number of Christians had increased to about 60 million, with Catholics and Protestants making up 50 million, and the other 10 million divided between the Ethiopian Orthodox and Coptic Churches. By 2005, the African Christian population had increased to roughly 393 million, which is just below 50 percent of Africa's population.[6]

Much of this extraordinary growth can be attributed directly to the Pentecostal-Charismatic outpouring, as the Spirit is moving mightily over the earth and a massive harvest of souls is being reaped. This is cause for rejoicing, adoration, and awe. The world has never seen the like before.

Allan Heaton Anderson begins his book *To the Ends of the Earth* by stating:

> Pentecostalism has experienced amazing growth from its humble beginnings with a handful of people at the beginning of the twentieth century to some half billion adherents at the end of the century. There are many reasons, but perhaps the most important is that it is fundamentally an "ends of the earth," missionary, polycentric, transnational religion. The experience of the Spirit and belief in world evangelization are hallmarks of Pentecostalism, and pentecostals believe that they are called to be witnesses for Jesus Christ to the farthest reaches of the globe in obedience to Christ's commission.

> And they have been remarkably successful. They have contributed enormously to the southward shift of Christianity's center of gravity and provided a powerful argument against the inevitability of secularization.[7]

Anderson then quotes the respected church historian John Philip Jenkins, who "speculates that pentecostal and independent churches will soon 'represent a far larger segment of global Christianity, and just conceivably a majority,' resulting in Pentecostalism being 'perhaps the most successful social movement of the past century.'"[8] Step back for a moment and read those words again. The impact of the Pentecostal outpouring is massive.

What makes this even more staggering is the fact that the early Pentecostals were mocked and ridiculed and cast out. Who could take such a bunch of spiritual misfits seriously? In the words of Rev. R. J. Burdette, who lived at the time of the Azusa Street Revival:

> As for new religions, beyond the numbering of a busy man, they come and go—especially in Los Angeles. They come with the blare of trumpets out of tune and harmony, but lustily blown with all the power of human or inhuman lungs; they shine with phosphorescent gleam, strangely, like that of brimstone, and with color more or less tainted; they distract the affrighted atmosphere with a bewildering jargon of babbling tongues of all grades—dried, boiled and soaked; they rant and jump and dance and roll in a disgusting amalgamation of African voodoo superstition and Caucasian insanity, and will pass away like the nightmares of hysteria that they are.[9]

Yes, the Azusa-type madness will soon disappear, just another example of these "nightmares of hysteria."

A secular newspaper carried this report, titled "Rolling on Floor in Smale's Church," mocking these early Pentecostal meetings:

> Muttering an unintelligible jargon, men and women rolled on the floor, screeching at the top of their voices at times, and again giving utterance to cries which resembled those of animals in pain. There was a Babel of sound. Men and women embraced each other in the fanatical orgy.... Suddenly [a fashionably dressed, pretty, young woman] arose and began to cackle like a hen. Forth and back she walked in front of the company, wringing her hands and clucking something which no one could interpret. The leader explained that she was speaking a dialect of a Hindoo [sic] tribe. He said she would leave soon for India to teach the natives the gospel.[10]

Other newspapers had a field day with the Azusa Street manifestations. Typical story lines included "Humane Society Is to Tackle Jumpers," "Whites and Blacks Mix in a Religious Frenzy," "Disgusting Scenes at Azusa Street Church," "How Holy Roller Gets Religion," "Holy Kickers Baptized 138," "Holy Rollers' Meetings Verge on Riot," and "Gifts of Tongues Works Havoc Among Churches." On one occasion it was alleged that, following a baptism on the beach, one man "so lacerated his neck with his fingernails while in a violent spasm that he bled a great deal. When he was carried away to the bathhouse the sand was discolored with blood."[11]

It is likely that some of these reports were completely bogus, while others were greatly exaggerated. But there's no question that the outpouring was highly unusual as well as far from perfect, so it was easy for critics to assail and assault, as they have also done with every revival movement in church history.[12] But it was from these humble, inauspicious, and even messy beginnings that a movement has grown that has brought more people into the kingdom of God than any other movement in world history. As Anderson notes:

> Facts and figures on the growth of any global religious movement are notoriously difficult to come by, yet statistics on the growth of Pentecostalism are exultingly quoted, especially by classical pentecostals. The most frequently quoted ones are those of Barrett and Johnson, who estimated that Pentecostalism had some 614 million adherents in 2010, a quarter of the world's Christian population, which they projected would rise to almost 800 million by 2025. This figure was placed at only 67 million in 1970, and this enormous increase has coincided with Europe's secularization zenith.[13]

The Spirit *is* moving mightily in the earth, and I am an eyewitness to this great outpouring, having ministered around the world on more than 150 overseas trips and having worked with some of the top Charismatic leaders in the United States and the nations.

At the same time, there are grave problems in our movement, because of which much compromise has entered our ranks, along with rampant moral scandals and a litany of doctrinal errors. Without a doubt, much of this is the result of the rapid growth of the movement, since an unprecedented number of souls has been saved in an extremely short period of time, resulting in many new converts, many ill-prepared leaders, and much immaturity. And it is true that revivals and revival movements can be quite untidy with all the emotion and upheaval and manifestations and responses. There will always be a mixture of the flesh and the Spirit, not to mention some satanic counterfeits along the way.

But this is not the time to make excuses. This is the time to grow up and clean house. As Jesus said, "To whom much is given...much shall be required (Luke 12:48). Surely much has been given to us.

As I will state elsewhere in this book, the finest men and women of God I have met on the planet are Pentecostals and Charismatics—men and women of the highest integrity, men and women of faith and prayer, men and women of godly character, men and women of devotion to the Word, men and women of courage and love and sacrifice. There is no shortage of saintly leaders and saintly believers in our movement. But there is also no shortage of abusive leaders (and even downright charlatans) as well as flaky believers, and it is to address these problems that I have written this book.

But I have not written this book as God's policeman or as judge and jury over His people. God forbid. Instead, I have written these pages with a deep sense of burden, with grief over the lives hurt because of uncorrected errors in our midst, and with pain because of the reproach that has been brought to the name of our Lord. I share His holy jealousy for His bride—in tiny measure, of course, compared with His passion—knowing how deeply He loves His people and how much He appreciates their sincere and simple faith. But there must be discernment with that faith, lest many lives be shipwrecked.

May a fresh awakening spread through our churches—an awakening of maturity and stability, an awakening worthy of the name of the Lord, an awakening worthy of the Spirit. Forward!

Chapter 2
Why Are We So Gullible?

A strong critic of the Charismatic movement forwarded a series of emails to me one day, all of them sent out by one Charismatic leader and all of them, quite obviously, designed to raise funds. One of the emails featured "the powerful, prophetic word the Lord has given specifically for YOU," followed by this appeal:

> Let your miracle harvest begin this very moment by sowing a seed of faith. When you sow seed, it can become a supernatural force and bring your miracles!
>
> Yes, this mass emailing has a personal, specific word for you, and if you give *us* your money, you will get your miracle![1]

Another email focused on Passover-Easter giving:

> Resurrection Seed is coming! This is the one season of the year that we see more miracles and blessings poured out than any other time—and I want you to receive the promise of SEVEN TIMES MORE!
>
> That's right. If you give *right now*, you will get seven times more than normal.

Then there was a follow-up email with an urgent and timely message:

> If you did not get the chance to sow your Passover offering—the deadline extension is about to end! Please

> sow now—place yourself in position to receive the seven anointings of Passover.

What kind of rubbish is this? There's a "deadline extension" on your giving, and it's about to end? Who exactly set the deadline and then extended it? And where does Scripture teach that there are "seven anointings of Passover," let alone that they are related to finances? Not only does this stuff bring reproach to the gospel; it also hurts sincere believers, many of whom will respond to these appeals. (Trust me on this: if these emails and letters didn't bring in the bucks, you wouldn't be getting them in your in-box or mailbox.)

The real question is, Why do Charismatic ministers have a virtual corner on this manipulative market? The answer, unfortunately, is that *we Charismatics are so gullible.* I can't imagine many non-Charismatics being duped by this kind of obvious spiritual manipulation.

Out of curiosity, I signed up to receive emails from a prophet who was known for using his gift for mercenary purposes. As expected, I received emails like this, announcing: "Your Check Date Is On Its Way! (Urgent Response Required)."[2]

The email continued:

> Dear Michael,
>
> I wrote you earlier and now there's [the] time is running out on your CHECK CASHING date…
>
> Michael,
>
> - **You've prayed for a financial breakthrough…**
> - **You've asked God to show up in your money…**
> - **You've been seeking a miracle in your finances…**

> After tomorrow, don't say the Prophet didn't tell once more about the LAW OF ABUNDANCE check because…
>
> - **There's a financial breakthrough God wants to release to you…**
> - **There's a golden opportunity to discover where your gold is…**
> - **There's a miracle money visitation that's in route…**
>
> (Your urgent response is required)
>
> The time has once again come and now it's reaching its critical point…
>
> **Time is running out on your** CHECK CASHING **date…**
>
> I won't do a song and dance to convince you of the importance of hearing God in this season because one missed opportunity can wreck [sic] havoc in your life…

He then gave examples of how people experienced financial loss and a lack of healing because they failed to heed his prophetic warnings. In other words, you could get sick or suffer serious loss if you don't send your check to the man of God today! He then cited 2 Chronicles 20:20 (stating that those who believe God's prophets will prosper) and closed with this lengthy appeal:

> CLICK HERE TO SOW THE $80.18 for DEUTERONOMY 8:18
>
> (Your urgent response is required)
>
> - MIRACLE MONEY is coming, discover WHEN now!
> - PROFITABLE CONNECTIONS are yours, discover WHO now!

- GOLDEN OPPORTUNITIES will be found, discover WHERE now!

CLICK HERE TO SOW THE $80.18 for DEUTERONOMY 8:18

Michael, here's what you must do now...

- **Locate your pen that you will write with when the instructions come on the audio I will send you! (immediately)**
- **Sow the Deut. 8:18 seed of $80.18 in obedience so I can get the audio to you immediately! (This is important)**
- **Await my new instructions for your dates!**

I must URGE you to avoid the cycle of missed opportunity and stop drowning in the sea of procrastination, which is the thief of time.

Nothing is more expensive than a missed opportunity! Don't miss your miracle!

CLICK HERE TO SOW THE $80.18 for DEUTERONOMY 8:18

I've been having multiple visions of partners known and unknown, counting 100 dollar bills that seemed to run endless. I also saw multiple new cars in all sorts of colors being driven off the car lots! There is a sea of abundance that is now SPRINGING FORTH and an unusual anointing of abundance has been on me strongly and I want you to understand that you don't want to miss this...

CLICK HERE TO SOW THE $80.18 for DEUTERONOMY 8:18

P.S. Michael, I am EXPECTING a windfall of new

> testimonies to come about during this appointed time for abundance. Borrow if you have to because you don't want to miss the dates that I will reveal to you in Jesus name! **Act NOW!**

As vile as this is, about one day later I received a follow-up email. Here's just the beginning of what the prophet sent:

> Dear Michael,
>
> **Do you have your check? It is time!** There's real power in this rhyme! I went before the Lord last night, and wrote you earlier to tell you. He showed the power of His might! He gave me dates for you to reap! Prosperity is your receipt! Do trust God's promise on your life... To give you wealth to rid your strife!
>
> Believe the Lord; it has its perks...
>
> - FAVOR shows and goes BESERK [sic]!
> - TIED UP MONIES get RELEASED!
> - FOES DISMANTLE FOR YOUR PEACE!
>
> But let him ask in faith, nothing wavering. For he that wavereth is like a wave of the sea driven with the wind and tossed...
>
> A double minded man is unstable in all his ways! (James 1:6–8)
>
> - **DON'T WAIVER [sic] in your mindset; pray!**
> - **DON'T WORRY that you'll miss your day!**
> - **DON'T DOUBT the prophet; that's absurd!**
> - **DON'T VOID what God brings by His word!**
> - **Your window of opportunity is open for the next 48 hours...**

- **DO YOU HAVE YOUR CHECK? IT'S TIME! I have instructions to align...you with ABUNDANCE and its LAW...through FAVOR you will be in AWE!**

I cannot begin to express how despicable this is in God's sight, yet it's not that uncommon in some of our circles. Perhaps some of you have seen even worse! And like spiritual robots programmed to respond to these manipulative, sinful appeals, we sit and write our checks for the amount requested. Talk about gullibility.

Some Other Questions to Ask

There are some other questions we could ask, including: 1) How much money do emails and letters like this bring in? 2) Were they even seen by the leader whose name the email carried, let alone written by him? 3) Why do so many of the prophetic words focus on supernatural financial blessing about to come your way—but only if you give to this specific ministry and only if you do it today? What happens if you give next month? Will you lose the sevenfold return? And what if you give that money to your local church instead? Will you not receive the promised supernatural blessing?

Some ministers plainly tell you that, no, you will not receive the same blessing if you give to your local church rather than to their ministries. Why? As one fund-raiser put it, "The anointing you sow into is the anointing you have a right to."

So if you give to your local church, which is just an average congregation and not particularly prosperous, then you can expect to receive an average, not particularly prosperous, return. But if you give to this super-anointed, super-powerful, super-prosperous ministry, you will receive a super-anointed, super-powerful, super-prosperous return.

With reasoning like that, it would be best to stay away from ministries that work with the suffering church. You might receive persecution in return! And you should certainly stay away from people like the apostle Paul. If you sow your finances into his work, you might end up in jail as he did!

Do you see how ridiculous this line of thinking is? It is certainly without biblical support. Giving to a ministry is not like buying a membership to a local country club. But that's the way it's pitched by the ministry's marketing team, and that's why it sells so well: share in our success by giving to us today.

Do I believe that some ministries are truly "good ground" and God will bless you for sowing into them? Yes, I do, because they're doing important work that is near and dear to God's heart. But the idea that you get to sow into some kind of special, financial miracle anointing is completely bogus and manipulative.

As for our gullibility, I find it remarkable that there are leaders who were caught in fraudulent activities yet continue to have financially prosperous ministries today, still drawing large audiences and still bringing in enough funds to keep them on TV. One such leader claimed to receive divine revelation about people in the audience, but it turned out that his wife was feeding him information through a hidden earpiece. This same leader recently offered a "Miracle Spring Water and Debt Cancelling Kit" to his supporters.[3] I can only imagine what the kit contained.

Some years back one of my colleagues started getting fundraising letters from a preacher in New York. He had no idea why he was receiving them, until he learned that one of his friends put him on this man's mailing list as a prank. After some time the preacher died, but that didn't stop the letters from coming. In fact, one of them came with a shower cap, on the outside of which was a life-size image of the departed man of God's right hand.

This way, when you put the shower cap on, he would be laying his anointed hand on you. I kid you not!

Interestingly, Paul was concerned about the gullibility of the Corinthians, since they were so easily duped by the false apostles. He wrote:

> I wish you would bear with me in a little foolishness. Do bear with me! For I feel a divine jealousy for you, since I betrothed you to one husband, to present you as a pure virgin to Christ. But I am afraid that as the serpent deceived Eve by his cunning, your thoughts will be led astray from a sincere and pure devotion to Christ. For if someone comes and proclaims another Jesus than the one we proclaimed, or if you receive a different spirit from the one you received, or if you accept a different gospel from the one you accepted, you put up with it readily enough.
>
> —2 Corinthians 11:1–4, esv

Now, it's true that there are warnings against deception throughout the Bible, and there are plenty of non-Charismatics who get duped as well. It just seems that we Charismatics are more prone to gullibility. Why? Interestingly there's a positive answer to this question as well as a negative one, and if we can better understand the positive, we can better avoid the negative.

On the positive side, we Charismatics really do believe God, and we've seen Him move and speak in unusual ways. (It's not just in our experience that we've seen the unusual. It's throughout the Word as well.) We're also trusting of our leaders, sometimes too trusting. Plus, the Lord in His mercy often honors our faith, even when we've been duped, blessing us for our sincerity despite the false promises of the ministry into which we sowed. So it looks as if the gimmick actually worked, making us think it will work next time.

Part of our gullibility, then, goes back to something that is precious in God's sight, namely, a childlike faith where we simply take Him at His Word. After all, who would have believed the gospel story if it weren't written in Scripture? Some people think we're crazy for believing that almighty God decided to save humanity through a crucified, resurrected Jewish carpenter. To the natural mind, the story does sound quite far-fetched. But we know it's true as surely as we know our own names. Why, then, shouldn't we believe some preacher today who makes a seemingly outlandish claim? Perhaps he too is telling the truth.

Look at the modern history of Israel for another example of an apparently impossible story. Who would have believed toward the end of World War II, with the ovens of the concentration camps still burning and two-thirds of European Jewry—six million out of nine million European Jews[4]—wiped out, that just three years later the State of Israel would be born? Who among us would have believed a prophet saying this would happen in 1945? Probably few, if any, of us.

I have come back from ministering in India with stories that defy belief, yet they're true, and I witnessed them myself. Why shouldn't I believe God when He speaks something to me today that seems outlandish and far-fetched?

In the late 1970s, Nancy and I heard a couple sharing about the Lord's miraculous provision in their lives. They had a show on Christian TV, and they smiled throughout their entire message, without ever changing their expression. At one point I turned to Nancy and said, "I wish they would stop smiling!" Everything seemed artificial.

As for their message, there's only one thing I remember about it. They said they were reduced to their last chicken, with no money to buy any more food. So they ate the chicken to the bones for dinner, but rather than throwing out the skeleton, they put it back in the refrigerator, praying for a miracle. Lo and behold, they said that every night for weeks (or months?) when they opened the refrigerator in the morning, all the meat was back on the bones, and they had another chicken for dinner.

You might say, "Nobody in their right mind would believe something so silly," and part of me agrees. Who can possibly believe this story? (We were certainly skeptical when we heard it.) On the other hand, how different is this from ravens bringing Elijah food every day? (See 1 Kings 17.) Or how different is this from a cat laying a fish at the door of a destitute Chinese Christian woman whose husband was in prison for his faith? According to a good friend, who was told this by a closely related source, this happened during the time he was locked up.

When my friends and I were first saved, lots of remarkable things happened, including one unusual food miracle. My two best friends and fellow band members, both of whom came to faith right before me, used to eat regularly at a deli in our small town, and they each had favorite sandwiches they would have prepared in a very particular, unusual way. One night they left my house late, well after the deli was closed, but they were hungry. As they got to an intersection in our small town, there in the middle of the road, right between the yellow lines, was a neatly folded brown bag. Intrigued, they picked up the bag and looked inside. To their astonishment, inside that bag were their two favorite sandwiches, each one prepared to their very specific tastes, cleanly wrapped, and totally fresh. With thanksgiving to God, they ate those sandwiches. What are the odds of something like that just "happening"? How many trillions to one?

During that same period of time, one of our friends in school was apparently born again, to our absolute joy and surprise. He and his twin brother were heavy drinkers and drug users, and they were tough cookies on top of that, getting into lots of fights. But for a short period of time, it seemed as if he really changed. He was at our house one night when he ripped his thumb on a piece of wood, and it was a real mess. A big chunk of flesh was missing, and there was an ugly gash. Of course we prayed for him since he was in pain, though we weren't necessarily expecting an outright miracle. But his faith was very much alive, and to our astonishment, when we saw him next (just a day or two later!), his thumb was perfectly fine, as if nothing at all had happened. There was no gash, and there was no scar. I saw it with my own eyes. He was stunned as well.

Why, then, shouldn't we believe the story of the chicken miracle? I'm not saying I do believe it; God knows the truth. I'm simply asking, On what basis should we *not* believe it? According to what Scripture? Based on what biblical principle? *Remember, discernment is not the same thing as skepticism, and cynicism is not a fruit of the Spirit.*

On July 31, 1998, a godly Christian woman was visiting the ministry school I was leading, and she had a prophetic word for me, part of which said I would stand before princes, something that had never crossed my mind. Less than two weeks later, on August 12, I was invited to a private one-hour meeting in Buckingham Palace with Prince Andrew, where I shared my testimony with him and prayed for him before I left. The meeting was initiated from start to finish by a colleague of mine, and to be candid, talking face-to-face with the prince was the furthest thing from my mind on that ministry trip to England. In fact, it was no more on my mind than meeting Elvis Presley, and it was only sometime after the meeting that I remembered the prophetic word. Why, then, should I be skeptical of other prophecies that seem highly unlikely?

A pastor in Kansas City told me about a word he received from a respected prophet, saying that when his church hit 180 people, "the explosion will come." This was a new church plant, but the pastor held on to that word, waiting for the spiritual explosion when they reached 180 people. One Sunday morning, they put out 182 chairs, and the pastor happened to notice that all the chairs were filled except two. Later that afternoon, when the building was empty, a gas line ruptured, and the building exploded. There was a literal explosion! No one was hurt, they were able to get into a bigger and better building, and they saw significant growth after that. Again, I heard this firsthand.

This same prophet was involved in an even stranger story. At another church on a Sunday morning, during a quiet time in worship, he shouted out, "Macaroni and cheese!" The pastor was shocked, the people were dismayed, and some wondered, "What did he just say? Was he so hungry that he couldn't wait for lunch?" To make matters worse, at that moment a visiting family stood up and walked out. He had offended these visitors with this silly word—or so the people thought.

A few months later, on a Sunday morning, that same family returned to the church, led by the very regal, godly mother. She asked if she could share a testimony, and the pastor gave her permission. She explained that the Lord told her to return to that church that morning to "vindicate the man of God," so she gathered her family and said, "We're going back to that church today."

It turns out that she had five children, four of whom were actively serving the Lord and one of whom was totally away from God, and she had been praying for confirmation that he would, in fact, return to the Lord. She felt led to attend that church for the first time a few months earlier, and when the worship got quiet, the prophet shouted out, "Macaroni and cheese!"

Well, that was the sign she needed, since *her son's job was delivering boxes of macaroni and cheese*, and she took the prophet's words as a sign that the Lord had His eyes on her boy. Having heard the words "macaroni and cheese," she felt that her mission was accomplished that morning, which is why she then left the service with her family. In the following months her son had come back to Jesus in dramatic fashion, and she wanted everyone to know what had happened.

I know it sounds crazy, but it happened, as have other things even more extreme and seemingly absurd. Why, then, shouldn't we believe the latest prophetic word?[5] The answer is simple: *It is because the Word of God tells us not to believe every spirit but to test the spirits.* The Bible frequently warns us against deception and tells us to beware of false prophets and false teachers. This means that being childlike in our faith does not mean being naive. Gullibility is no more a fruit of the Spirit than skepticism.

Why, then, are we so undiscerning? Why are we so quick to believe anything and everything so long as the right "spiritual" language is used? Why are we so gullible?

Think of men such as Abraham, Elijah, Daniel, Peter, and Paul. They were men of great faith, but they were anything but gullible. They believed what *the Spirit* said, not what *any spirit* said. They knew the difference between a word from above and a word from below, the difference between their human emotions and the leading of the Lord.

It's the same with some of the great Pentecostal pioneers, such as Smith Wigglesworth or John G. Lake. Read their messages, and you will see men who stepped out in radical obedience to the Lord, often doing highly unusual things. For example, a South African pastor related how Wigglesworth, who was there in the 1930s,[6] was taking a prayer walk through a very nice neighborhood one day when he heard the Lord say to him, "Go to the front door of that house and yell the words of John 3:16 through the keyhole."

Wigglesworth said to the Lord, "I could never do that. It would be a scandal!" But he knew the voice of his Master too well, and the Lord spoke to him with real force and urgency. So Wigglesworth ran up to the door, shouted the words of John 3:16 through the keyhole, then ran back to the street.

At the Wigglesworth meeting that night a very well-dressed man showed up, asking if he could testify. Just that afternoon, he said, only a few hours ago, he was standing on a chair in his living room with a rope around his neck, ready to commit suicide, when suddenly he heard someone shout John 3:16 through his door. He was stunned by this message from God, decided not to kill himself, and had to attend the gospel meeting that night. Little did he know the man conducting the meeting was the man who yelled, "For God so loved the world" through his door!

But Wigglesworth was anything but gullible. He literally lived in the Word, reportedly never going fifteen minutes without either quoting the Scriptures or reading them, and the Bible was the only book he read his entire life.[7] He was a believer, not a fool.

The same can be said of Lake, who was a great scientific thinker and even conducted experiments with doctors at the Mayo Clinic to see how brain waves were affected by speaking in tongues, among other things. At the beginning of this ministry, based on a word from the Lord, he left a lucrative career, sold everything he had, and traveled to South Africa with his wife and seven children, without a dime of support and without a known ministry connection waiting for him when he arrived. His five years of ministry there, before his wife's death, literally impacted the nation.[8]

But Lake too was anything but gullible. He was mature in his faith, having learned to distinguish the voice of God and the leading of God from all other voices and leadings. Why can't we do the same? Why are we so easily led astray?

A good friend of mine from the States served on the mission field in Europe for over forty years, and he would always be stunned to come back to America and discover the latest Charismatic fad. "Where in the world did *this* come from?" he would wonder. Soon enough, it would spread to other Charismatic ministries around the world, only to be replaced by the newest and latest fad. He could only shake his head and sigh.

A church in South Korea seemed to have a major breakthrough in deliverance ministry, seeing many people freed from demonic strongholds. This certainly sounds scriptural, and it's surprising that all of us are not more actively involved in driving out demons. In this church, on a regular basis, unclean spirits were leaving people in very dramatic ways, shouting and crying out as they left. (For the record, I've witnessed some remarkable deliverances too.)

Was it all genuine? Perhaps so, but I wasn't there and can't say. What I do know, however, is that those casting out the demons decided to start asking them questions, thinking that these devilish beings had inside information into the spirit realm. After all, they knew what was really happening behind the scenes, right? They even knew Satan's exact strategies! And wasn't it the demons in the Gospels that confessed that Jesus is the Son of God?

Before long this church started sharing this newly acquired information, even changing some of its doctrines. Those from the church had discovered a new method of gaining supernatural revelation, asking the demons questions and taking their words as truth. How crazy! Can you imagine having the devil and his minions as your spiritual guides and teachers?

But this is just another example of extreme gullibility and lack of discernment. Some of us will believe just about anything. In this case, rather than test the spirits in order to *recognize* demonic revelation, they tested the spirits in order to *receive* demonic revelation. Talk about a deluded and dangerous wild-goose chase.

On a regular basis, Charismatic critics ask me about the practice of "grave soaking" (or "grave sucking"). This refers to believers lying on the graves of departed men and women of God in order to "soak in" (or "suck up") their anointings or mantles. So just as the bones of Elisha brought resurrection to a man thrown into his grave (2 Kings 13:20–21), the graves of departed saints are thought to carry anointings or mantles that can be transmitted. Leave it to us Charismatics to devise a practice like this.

Now, it's true that leaders of the major ministry often blamed for this practice categorically denounced it, saying it was nothing they ever taught or modeled. So it is erroneous to accuse this ministry of aiding or abetting this practice. And I have no problem with praying at the gravesite of a departed leader for the purpose of sober reflection, even asking God to impart some of what He imparted to that person. But the idea that by lying on a godly person's gravesite we can suck up his mantle or anointing—what can I say? Such a practice deserves to be ridiculed. This may even border on consulting with the dead.

I recently watched a video of a pastor in Africa who claimed that God gave him His personal phone number. That's right. This pastor claimed to have a literal direct line to heaven, and on this video that I watched, he took out his cell phone, dialed a number, and asked, "Is this heaven?" (I'm not making this up.) He then purported to talk to God on his phone, relaying the information he received to his congregants, who seemed quite excited by this new development.

His congregation, of course, was Charismatic, something I assumed before I watched the video. Who else would believe such nonsense? I say this to our shame.

Perhaps this pastor knows another African leader who claims

that after being taken up to heaven, he took pictures there. And yes, you guessed it. You can buy those heavenly shots for a suitable donation.[9] And how about the African pastor who claims to be able to walk on the air?[10]

I've been told that some pastors in Africa have purchased so-called holy oil from India, blessed by a guru with alleged healing powers, and they are selling it at exorbitant prices to their congregations. Ironically I was also told some pastors in *India* have purchased so-called holy water from *Israel* and are sprinkling it on people for healing, using it for financial gain as well. Does this ever stop?

But it gets worse. It is reliably reported that some African pastors have worked with witch doctors, partnering with their demonic powers to grow their churches, to the point that one popular witch doctor claims that he "backs up" over 1,700 African preachers annually. There was even a scandal that became very public when a witch doctor claimed he had made a deal with a famous pastor in his city. He says he agreed to bury an item at the entrance to the church that would then supernaturally draw people into the building, and he and the pastor split the offerings collected. Allegedly, they had this arrangement for years but then had a falling out, at which time the witch doctor went public, apparently with damning evidence.

The good news is that other Christian leaders in the region refused to work with this pastor, repudiating his orthodoxy. The bad news is that such a thing ever took place and that the man's ministry continues to this day.

To be fair, throughout Africa there are fine Christian leaders who put many of us in the West to shame. In fact, some of them have been sent as missionaries to the United States and Europe, and they are doing amazing works for the Lord.

I think immediately of a pastor from Ghana who has served

in Germany more than twenty-six years and is seeing incredible results in his ministry to Muslims. I interviewed him on a recent trip to Germany, and I was stirred to hear him preach Jesus with such boldness and faith. No wonder he has personally baptized *more than one thousand ex-Muslims in the last decade.*

Some of the finest saints you'll ever meet are African and Indian. But with the rapid spread of the gospel in those regions, there are many abuses that must be addressed as well.

Back in the States, one leader sent me a list of Charismatic abuses she's addressed publicly in the last couple of years, including:

- A Colorado group that "invites 'students of the Word' to inhale weed, ganja, marijuana, pot—or whatever the going slang for the depressant drug is these days—while they hash out what the Lord is trying to say through the Scripture." And boy do the revelations flow! One woman was surprised with the results: "I expected to see unicorns. But when I started smoking I just got so connected to God."[11] It would have been better if she had seen unicorns.

- Another prophet sent out a fund-raising email, explaining that the Lord showed him he had been making a spiritual mistake, which is why he didn't have enough money for his ministry bills. And what was his mistake? "With over $100,000 in financial endeavors," he wrote, "I have been holding on to your breakthrough by keeping this a secret from you. You see, when a prophet is in a season of famine, God is looking to release to those who would lift him out of the famine, a miracle of breakthrough." So that was it. He was in debt because he was wrongfully holding on to your breakthrough by not asking you to give him money! But of course! Indeed, "As your personal prophet, it is unlawful for me to hold onto your breakthrough!" And how much was "your personal prophet" asking for? No need to wonder at all: "If you stand with me with the $397 donation, I will send you an MP3 or CD (CD upon request) with the company of prophets and myself speaking a word of breakthrough into your situation for the next twelve months."[12] What a deal!

- A Seattle, Washington-based man "used deceptive practices to wring about $7.75 million out of the desperate hands of 165,000 customers seeking God's divine intervention in their circumstances." How did the scam work? A so-called prayer center "sold intercession for between $9 to $35 for each petition via a website that is now shut down," among other abuses.[13] And 165,000 poor souls fell for it.
- And here's one more from Africa: a prophet in South Africa encouraged his church members to drink Dettol, a potentially lethal disinfectant, in order to receive a healing. He claims God instructed him to do it, and he obeyed, drinking the poisonous disinfectant before giving it to his congregants to drink. And drink it they did.[14]

Is it any surprise that our critics mock us so savagely? And is it any surprise that true seekers get scandalized by abuses such as these—abuses that are all too common? Perhaps some of these are a bit more extreme, but there are many, many leaders taking advantage of Charismatic gullibility and padding their own bank accounts in the process. Isn't it high time for this to be confronted? If we would just exercise the smallest amount of discernment—such as stopping for a moment to think and pray before responding—we would stop falling for these gimmicks, quickly putting these hucksters, charlatans, and misleading leaders out of business.

Enough with our foolish gullibility. May a spirit of true, mature faith arise, and may we stop acting like little children. It's time to be men and women of God.

Chapter Three
Mercenary Prophets

While working on a commentary on the Book of Jeremiah, I studied the prophet's words for several years, almost day and night. I felt as if I got to know Jeremiah personally, understanding his heart, feeling his burden, sharing his pain, entering into his battles. And what battles he had, especially with the false prophets and priests.

More than twenty-five hundred years ago Jeremiah delivered this word of rebuke from the Lord: "For from the least to the greatest of them, everyone is greedy for unjust gain; and from prophet to priest, everyone deals falsely. They have healed the wound of my people lightly, saying, 'Peace, peace,' when there is no peace" (Jer. 6:13–14, ESV). These prophets tell you what you want to hear, not what you need to hear, since their goal is to make money through their religious services. They do it by tickling people's ears rather than by telling them the truth.

Is it any surprise? How much money do you think you would make by exposing people's sins? If you called for repentance, how long would the line of people be waiting to receive a personal prophecy from you?

Commenting on Jeremiah 6:13–14, I wrote, "And so, it could easily be argued that as Jerusalem lay in ruins with the temple burning in its midst—its economy ruined, its people scattered or killed, its glory turned to shame—it was the prophets' love of money that helped ignite that unquenchable conflagration."[1] That is a staggering thought.

Micah too confronted this same corrupt spirit: "Thus says the

LORD concerning the prophets who lead my people astray, who cry 'Peace' when they have something to eat, but declare war against him who puts nothing into their mouths" (Micah 3:5, ESV; the Hebrew is literally "consecrate war," which could be translated "launch a crusade" or "declare a holy war"). Give them a good offering, and you're sure to get a good word. Don't pay them for their prophecy, and they'll launch a crusade against you.

So this manipulative, mercenary use of God's gift is nothing new. It's been a plague ever since the days of Balaam, if not before. (See Numbers 22–24.)

One of my colleagues ministers extensively overseas, and he told me about a heartbreaking situation he has encountered in one particular nation. There are prophets who charge an exorbitant fee to give you an alleged personal word from the Lord—he told me the fee is equivalent to a year's income—and people stand in long lines waiting to get their word. These prophets, who also pastor churches, have become so rich that they have bought extensive airtime to broadcast their meetings on TV, drawing large numbers to their congregations, to the great consternation of the authentic pastors.

So these men are sinning by charging for the exercising of a spiritual gift—Who gave them the right to sell what the Lord freely gave them?—and they are adding to their sin by making the fee so high they bankrupt God's people for their own personal profit. They then go even further by using some of their riches to broadcast their message on TV, and I can assure you, it is not a pure gospel message. But they thus dominate the airwaves, which then increases their congregations, bringing in further income. Talk about a ministry scam!

Peter rebuked Simon the sorcerer in Acts 8:20 for thinking the gift of God could be bought with money. *These mercenary prophets think the gift of God can be sold.*

Years after Peter encountered Simon, he rebuked the false prophets and false teachers of his day, saying, "They commit adultery with their eyes, and their desire for sin is never satisfied. They lure unstable people into sin, and they are well trained in greed. They live under God's curse. They have wandered off the right road and followed the footsteps of Balaam son of Beor, who loved to earn money by doing wrong. But Balaam was stopped from his mad course when his donkey rebuked him with a human voice" (2 Pet. 2:14–16, NLT). These contemporary frauds need to be rebuked as well.

It's possible that some of these men are relying on demonic powers to give people personal prophecies, just like the slave girl in Acts 16, who used a spirit of divination. It's also possible they are master manipulators who read people for a living, raking in the bucks through human guile. But it's possible that they have a genuine gift from God—remember, His gifts and callings are irrevocable (Rom. 11:29)—and that they are prostituting something sacred from heaven. That, to me, would be the most grievous thing of all.

If you have a hard time believing that the Lord would allow His gifts to be abused like that, consider the story of Samson. In Judges 16 he sleeps with a Philistine prostitute, violating two divine commands. First, he committed fornication. Second, he did it with a pagan woman. And this is while he was the national leader of Israel.

But look at what happens next. Here's the complete account:

> Samson went to Gaza, and there he saw a prostitute, and he went in to her. The Gazites were told, "Samson has come here." And they surrounded the place and set an ambush for him all night at the gate of the city. They kept quiet all night, saying, "Let us wait till the light of

> the morning; then we will kill him." But Samson lay till midnight, and at midnight he arose and took hold of the doors of the gate of the city and the two posts, and pulled them up, bar and all, and put them on his shoulders and carried them to the top of the hill that is in front of Hebron.
>
> —Judges 16:1–3, ESV

This passage really puts the fear of God in me. Samson wakes up from sleeping with a pagan prostitute and then rips the doors of the city gate right out of the ground and carries them on his shoulders. He still had his supernatural strength. The gift still operated. His sin did not stop the Spirit's empowerment. And the only thing that ultimately stopped the gift was his violating the divine covenant, which required him not to cut his hair.

Deceiving the Flock

A former student of mine, whom we'll call Alan, was a member of a Charismatic Lutheran church, and his pastor was a dynamic preacher. One Wednesday night Alan was deeply moved by the pastor's message, and he, along with many other congregants, responded to the altar call with tears. What an anointed word!

Days later Alan was shocked to hear what had happened immediately before that service. The church board had called for a meeting with the pastor to confront him with charges that he was living in adultery. He denied the charges adamantly, rebuking the board members for even entertaining such claims, and left the meeting in a huff. He went straight from that board meeting to the church service and proceeded to preach an incredibly moving message.

Yet it turns out he *was* guilty of adultery, and he had lied through his teeth to those board members. Still, he was able to turn on his preaching skills like a paid performer, to the point that his congregants couldn't tell something was amiss.

Alan was disappointed in himself, feeling he should have sensed in his heart that something wasn't right. But what if this pastor's preaching gift was still operating? That's a scary thought, and that's why the Samson story is so disturbing to me. You can be living in sin and still flow in the gifts, adding to your self-deception and allowing you to deceive the flock. *I would hate to be in such a person's shoes on that great day of accounting.* God does not take it lightly when His servants abuse His flock and mock His Spirit.

A sister who was involved with a house of prayer in her city wrote to me, grieved over what she was seeing. She asked, "What are we to do? Just follow unscrupulous false prophets because they still have the power gifts flowing freely? Just allow the charlatan-like prophets to steal every penny from the poor because their message sounds right and their gifts are still flowing?"

A Charismatic critic emailed me a couple of years back, pleading with me to watch a segment from a recent broadcast of a famous TV preacher. I watched, and I was shocked. The critic was not exaggerating. This prominent leader brought a prophet onto his program and asked him to receive the offering. The prophet claimed to have received a direct, clear word from the Lord warning of a major disaster coming that September, which was then just a few weeks off. The good news was that if you gave an offering of $500, you, your children, and your grandchildren would be protected from this disaster, plus your debts would be cancelled and your body healed. And this was on national (and probably international) Christian TV.

How in the world did the stations allow this to air? And how could this prominent leader allow this to happen on his watch? (I imagine he was quite pleased with it, to be candid.) This is absolutely corrupt in every way.

Aside from the fact that no major disaster happened that September, it is complete manipulation to claim people must give a sacrificial gift to a particular ministry to be protected from a disaster. What if they simply trusted God to protect them from this impending doom? And what if they could only afford to give $250? Does that mean only half of their family would be protected? Yet people wrote out their checks and donated their hard-earned money, believing the smooth talk of this slick prophet. I'd be surprised if he didn't receive a nice cut of the offering too.

This same prophet also spoke at a megachurch, asking the congregants to sow $49 into his ministry. If they did so, he assured them, their cupboards would not be bare when famine comes to our land.

You say, "But it's obvious he's not a prophet, since that prophesied disaster never came." The problem is that he has had other words come to pass, and he has a certain aura about him, so the sheep are duped into believing whatever he says. Is he just a slick operator, or is he abusing a gift? Either way, this is grave and ugly, and he too will have much accounting to do at the throne of God one day. Yet he is still preaching to crowds, he still has a large following on social media, and I'm sure he's still bringing in the bucks. It would give me great joy to know by the time this book is published that he had deeply and truly repented.

The same woman who expressed her concern about "charlatan-like prophets" detailed what she encountered at a conference featuring this same man.

> I was skeptical at first about the...conference because not only did they charge you for the conference, which was only $20, not a bad price, but they required a $100

> donation to go into the special prophecy room. I myself am a prophet and a missionary and have prophesied over many, perhaps even thousands, over the years. I never charge anything and very rarely take up offerings and never for myself.

So this woman believes in prophetic ministry and has prophesied over others without ever charging anyone to receive a word. (Honestly, the thought of charging someone for a word boggles my mind.) Yet at this conference the fee was $100 to get into the "special prophecy room." Talk about mercenary ministry.

She continued:

> Having said that, I watched as night after night, the offerings increased, until the last night at the conference there were six offerings collected—it took four hours to do this!—and then there was 30 minutes to an hour of ministry late at night. They spent the entire weekend talking about how Prophet [X] was perfect in all his ways. I had never met or seen Prophet [X] before, so I had no preconceived ideas, except that many admired him and said he was the true prophet. On the other hand, I went into the prophecy rooms, and the unknown lady who prayed for me was absolutely spot-on.

Everything in this description is wrong: more and more pleading for money, less and less teaching of the Word, and the exaltation of a flawed human vessel. Yet the prophetic gift was still flowing through an "unknown lady." Again, that is a scary thought. In the midst of such a compromised environment a genuine spiritual gift appeared to be in operation.

This sister ended by saying this:

> I came away from this conference really grieved and wondering about the mixture that I had watched and that I had experienced. I even was coerced into giving an offering, as he declared the Holy Spirit told him what and how much to ask for. Then at one point he asked if those who had spent their last hundred dollars to come to this conference would come up front. About 300 people came forward. I thought he was going to return their money to them; I hoped so. He actually said if they would donate that last hundred dollars, God would bless them, and he took it from them. At that point I fell on my knees weeping in intercession and begging the Lord to forgive the body of Christ for this gross misuse. I wept for a long time.

The striking thing here is that, with all the massive red flags and with all the abuses, this woman still felt "coerced" into giving an offering. She too got duped, despite years of ministry experience. That's the kind of pressure these mercenary ministers put on people, and sadly these professional prophets know what buttons to push to get sincere believers to do stupid things. God forbid that we grieve the Spirit and fail to do what the prophet says![2]

Spiritual Extortionists

One night I flipped on a Christian TV show, only to see a well-known fund-raiser preaching a powerful message on Jesus in the Garden of Gethsemane. I had seen him once or twice before, using the biblical feasts to raise large offerings. (This has become quite a fad these days. As I pointed out in the previous chapter, we're told that if we give on certain days of the years, such as the Day of Atonement, we will receive supernatural miracles of all kinds.) I said to myself, "There's no way he's going to take something as sacred as the agony of our Lord in Gethsemane and turn it into a fund-raising trick. He couldn't do that."

Sure enough, he did. I was sick to my stomach and had to turn the TV off immediately. What kind of person uses the Savior's suffering to bilk God's people of their money? Has he no conscience?

One of my friends knows this brother personally and told me he's very sincere, he's a great pastor, and he genuinely believes in what he's doing. That makes it even more pathetic to me. It's one thing if you're a total charlatan living a double life, preaching for money one day and partying with the world the next. That is bad enough. But in this case the manipulative fund-raiser was said to be a committed pastor. What else could he justify in the name of the Lord? And to repeat my previous question: How much money does he take home when he brings in the bucks for the Christian network?

As former *Charisma* editor Lee Grady wrote:

> Greed has actually morphed into a virtue in some charismatic circles, where pastors take hourlong offerings and guest speakers require limousines and five-figure honorariums to maintain their celebrity lifestyles. It's especially bad on some Christian TV channels, where spiritual extortionists sell medieval-style indulgences disguised as "Day of Atonement offerings" and use other ridiculous ploys to rob Christians. God, give us leaders who hate dishonest gain![3]

I was staying at a pastor's home years ago when he told me about an experience he had with a prophetic minister. This brother had preached at his church and ministered prophetically, and the meetings went well overall. He then learned that the church owed $400,000 on its building fund, and he made a proposal to the pastor. "I have a gift for raising funds," he said, "and I have faith that if you let me raise an offering, we can bring in the entire $400,000 in one night." (The church had perhaps six hundred members at most, so this would have been quite an amazing offering.)

This got the pastor's attention since this prophet seemed to be very sincere. "The only thing I ask for," the guest speaker said, "is 10 percent of what comes in."

The pastor replied, "Well, I have a problem with that since if we raise $400,000, then we have to pay you $40,000, in which case we haven't paid off the debt. And if I tell the people we need $440,000 so we can pay you too, then I've changed the amount of money we owe. So thanks but no thanks." Needless to say, he did not invite this man back.

But again, the scary thing is that this speaker might have had a real fund-raising gift—a gift of supernatural faith—yet he was using it for personal financial gain. On the other hand, he may simply have been a master manipulator. Either way, it was all yours for a handsome fee. When will this garbage stop?

Paul wrote to the Corinthians, "You see, we are not like the many hucksters who preach for personal profit. We preach the word of God with sincerity and with Christ's authority, knowing that God is watching us" (2 Cor. 2:17, NLT). This was an issue in Paul's day, just as it was in Old Testament times. As for Paul and his colleagues, they were aware that God was watching them, which begs the question "Have today's mercenary prophets no fear of the Lord?"

Perhaps some of them were trained by other corrupt leaders and for them this is the normal way of doing things. After all, I've heard it argued, in Bible days you wouldn't dare approach a prophet without bringing some kind of gift. (See, for example, 1 Samuel 9:6–7 and 1 Kings 14:3.) So why think you can go to a prophet for guidance today without bringing a financial gift? The answers are not hard to find.

First, these prophets did not charge for their services. Some contemporary prophets do. Second, people would bring a gift of appreciation to the man of God, such as a loaf of bread. This was out of respect and helped supply his day-to-day needs. There was no fee required, and in most cases in the Bible there's no mention of a gift being given. Third, the prophet would not be getting rich off the gifts of the people. As we saw at the outset of this chapter, ministering for money was strongly condemned by the true prophets, and priestly and prophetic greed was rebuked and exposed. Fourth, charging for prophecy is just as ungodly as charging for healing. Show me one place in the Bible where a leader required a payment before praying for the sick. (For an example of a prophet refusing payment after a healing, see 2 Kings 5, especially vv. 15–16, and then read to the end of the chapter.)

As I've stated many times, I believe in supporting God's servants, and as someone who has been in full-time ministry for decades, I appreciate the generosity of God's people. But there is a massive difference between helping to meet the legitimate needs of a ministry and getting rich off the gospel, especially by prostituting a spiritual gift.

Samuel himself testified to the nation:

> "I have walked before you from my youth until this day. Here I am; testify against me before the LORD and before his anointed. Whose ox have I taken? Or whose donkey have I taken? Or whom have I defrauded? Whom have I oppressed? Or from whose hand have I taken a bribe to blind my eyes with it? Testify against me and I will restore it to you."
>
> They said, "You have not defrauded us or oppressed us

> or taken anything from any man's hand." And he said to them, "The LORD is witness against you, and his anointed is witness this day, that you have not found anything in my hand."
>
> And they said, "He is witness."
>
> —1 SAMUEL 12:2–5, ESV

Samuel's integrity spoke for itself. He did not use his gift and calling to get rich off God's people.

A Sobering Warning

Here is a strong word of warning to every minister of the gospel who is manipulating the Lord's flock for personal gain. (And please don't tell me that you're only doing it because you want to see the people blessed. If that's the case, then sow the money they give back into other ministries, especially those helping the poor, rather than putting it into your own pocket.) This is from 1 Samuel, and it was written shortly before the two men described here, who were the sons of Eli the high priest, died:

> Now the sons of Eli were worthless men. They did not know the LORD.
>
> The custom of the priests with the people was that when any man offered sacrifice, the priest's servant would come, while the meat was boiling, with a three-pronged fork in his hand, and he would thrust it into the pan or kettle or cauldron or pot. All that the fork brought up the priest would take for himself. This is what they did at Shiloh to all the Israelites who came there.
>
> Moreover, before the fat was burned, the priest's servant would come and say to the man who was sacrificing, "Give meat for the priest to roast, for he will not accept boiled meat from you but only raw."

> And if the man said to him, "Let them burn the fat first, and then take as much as you wish," he would say, "No, you must give it now, and if not, I will take it by force."
>
> Thus the sin of the young men was very great in the sight of the LORD, for the men treated the offering of the LORD with contempt.
>
> —1 SAMUEL 2:12–17, ESV

Note four important phrases here: 1) the sons of Eli were worthless men; 2) they did not know the Lord; 3) their sin was very great in the sight of the Lord; 4) they treated the offering of the Lord with contempt. *This is not a game you want to play.*

But there's more. These men were also sleeping with the women who served at the tent of meeting (1 Sam. 2:22)—there's frequently a connection between immorality and greed—and Eli rebuked them with this warning: "If someone sins against a man, God will mediate for him, but if someone sins against the LORD, who can intercede for him?" (1 Sam. 2:25, ESV). Yet the Lord held Eli responsible for allowing them to continue in their sin—Eli rebuked them, but he didn't stop them—and because of their sin he received a chilling word of rebuke. It is one of the most painful passages of judgment in the Bible, and I'm going to quote it here in full:

> And there came a man of God to Eli and said to him, "Thus says the LORD, 'Did I indeed reveal myself to the house of your father when they were in Egypt subject to the house of Pharaoh? Did I choose him out of all the tribes of Israel to be my priest, to go up to my altar, to burn incense, to wear an ephod before me? I gave to the house of your father all my offerings by fire from the people of Israel. Why then do you scorn my sacrifices and my offerings that I commanded for my dwelling, and

> honor your sons above me by fattening yourselves on the choicest parts of every offering of my people Israel?'
>
> "Therefore the LORD, the God of Israel, declares: 'I promised that your house and the house of your father should go in and out before me forever,' but now the LORD declares: 'Far be it from me, for those who honor me I will honor, and those who despise me shall be lightly esteemed. Behold, the days are coming when I will cut off your strength and the strength of your father's house, so that there will not be an old man in your house. Then in distress you will look with envious eye on all the prosperity that shall be bestowed on Israel, and there shall not be an old man in your house forever. The only one of you whom I shall not cut off from my altar shall be spared to weep his eyes out to grieve his heart, and all the descendants of your house shall die by the sword of men.
>
> "'And this that shall come upon your two sons, Hophni and Phinehas, shall be the sign to you: both of them shall die on the same day. And I will raise up for myself a faithful priest, who shall do according to what is in my heart and in my mind. And I will build him a sure house, and he shall go in and out before my anointed forever. And everyone who is left in your house shall come to implore him for a piece of silver or a loaf of bread and shall say, "Please put me in one of the priests' places, that I may eat a morsel of bread."'"
>
> —1 SAMUEL 2:27–36, ESV

Shortly after this word was given, Hophni and Phinehas were killed, the ark of the Lord was captured by the Philistines, and Eli himself was dead—all because these men, all priests, profaned the Lord's sacred things. To quote Paul's words from a relevant (but slightly different) context: "Now these things took place as examples for us, that we might not desire evil as they did.... Now these things happened to them as an example, but they were written down for our instruction, on whom the end of the ages has come. Therefore let anyone who thinks that he stands take heed lest he fall" (1 Cor. 10:6, 11–12, ESV).

I once heard a manipulative fund-raiser close his appeal by saying, "Lord, if anything I have said did not come straight from You, then let my tongue cleave to the roof of my mouth." I said to myself, "Perhaps the worst judgment of all would be that God would let him keep speaking."

Here, then, is a word of warning to every mercenary minister and every professional prophet from the Lord Jesus Himself: "For nothing is hidden that will not be made manifest, nor is anything secret that will not be known and come to light" (Luke 8:17, ESV). And, "I tell you, on the day of judgment people will give account for every careless word they speak, for by your words you will be justified, and by your words you will be condemned" (Matt. 12:36–37, ESV).

May God have mercy and grant repentance before it's too late.

Chapter Four
Superstar Leaders

There are some scholars who believe Paul's thorn, described in 2 Corinthians 12, referred to the false apostles that plagued him, especially in Corinth. I don't hold this view myself, but there's no doubt that these false apostles (he called them "super apostles") caused him many problems. Somehow their message (and persona) was especially appealing to the Corinthians.

It seems the believers in Corinth were impressed with big personalities and big talk. They were attracted to outward success and personal charisma. The way of the cross was not for them. They wanted to live like royalty: "Already you have all you want! Already you have become rich! Without us you have become kings! And would that you did reign, so that we might share the rule with you!" (1 Cor. 4:8, ESV). Paul and other apostles were not so lucky: "For I think that God has exhibited us apostles as last of all, like men sentenced to death, because we have become a spectacle to the world, to angels, and to men" (1 Cor. 4:9, ESV). Paul was not a superstar!

The Corinthians mistook Paul's sacrificial service for weakness, and because they were so focused on outward appearance and performance, they were not impressed with this mighty apostle. "His letters are weighty and strong," they said to themselves, "but his bodily presence is weak, and his speech of no account" (2 Cor. 10:10, ESV).

To repeat, Paul was not a superstar. Yet it was the superstar apostles who took advantage of the Corinthian believers, using

God's people for personal gain rather than serving them for their good. (Does this sound familiar?) Paul even had to write, "For I was not at all inferior to these super-apostles, even though I am nothing" (2 Cor. 12:11, ESV).

When it came time for Paul to boast about his apostleship, he listed his sufferings for the gospel, and it was quite an overwhelming list. Rather than skip over the following passage, please take a moment to read it slowly and carefully, feeling the full weight of Paul's words. He wrote:

> Are they servants of Christ? I am a better one—I am talking like a madman—with far greater labors, far more imprisonments, with countless beatings, and often near death. Five times I received at the hands of the Jews the forty lashes less one. Three times I was beaten with rods. Once I was stoned. Three times I was shipwrecked; a night and a day I was adrift at sea; on frequent journeys, in danger from rivers, danger from robbers, danger from my own people, danger from Gentiles, danger in the city, danger in the wilderness, danger at sea, danger from false brothers; in toil and hardship, through many a sleepless night, in hunger and thirst, often without food, in cold and exposure. And, apart from other things, there is the daily pressure on me of my anxiety for all the churches.
>
> Who is weak, and I am not weak? Who is made to fall, and I am not indignant? If I must boast, I will boast of the things that show my weakness. The God and Father of the Lord Jesus, he who is blessed forever, knows that I am not lying. At Damascus, the governor under King Aretas was guarding the city of Damascus in order to seize me, but I was let down in a basket through a window in the wall and escaped his hands.
>
> —2 CORINTHIANS 11:23–33, ESV

Paul was saying, "If you want to see what a real apostle looks like, look at me—at the things I have suffered, at the hardships I have experienced, at my weakness. And then look again at the signs, wonders, and miracles that God performed through me as I persevered without quitting by his grace." [See also 2 Corinthians 12:12, where Paul wrote, "The signs of a true apostle were performed among you with utmost patience, with signs and wonders and mighty works" (ESV).] In contrast, the super-apostles boasted in their strength, their abilities, their personalities, and their riches. And the Corinthians wanted to be like them!

Unfortunately we have an epidemic today of super-apostles (or, more broadly, superstar leaders), and in some circles it seems to be getting worse, not better. Let me share some experiences I've had in the United States and abroad. But let me also say this at the outset (and may the critics take note of this too): for every superstar leader I've known of firsthand, I know one hundred or one thousand who are anything but superstars. The finest leaders I know around the world—people of prayer, purity, passion, devotion, compassion, burden, conviction, sacrifice, service, and surrender—are Charismatic. Unfortunately a few bad apples make the others look bad, and a bad public witness gets more media attention than ten thousand fine private witnesses.

What I've Seen and Heard

I've had the privilege of ministering in Italy many times since 1987, earning a good reputation with the leaders there. When I arrived to minister one time, I learned that some of the pastors were very upset with the last speaker, a famous preacher from America. It almost made them suspicious of me, even though they had known me for years. They said, "He made all these promises about what would happen, but the only thing he left us with was a giant hotel bill." They were stunned by the money he spent while there, and he billed it all to them.

To be candid, some of these pastors could learn something about generosity and giving. But they had every right to be upset with the American preacher. What he did was abusive and unethical.

This same leader reputedly demanded a guarantee of $200,000 before agreeing to minister in a Third World country. He also allegedly demanded to be chauffeured in a Rolls-Royce while there. (I heard this from a well-connected, highly respected national leader in that country. He told me the organizers who invited him were very surprised and upset by his demands.)

One leader was reputed to stay in hotel rooms in the States that cost $20,000 per night. (I had no idea such rooms existed.) And it was money from God's people, including donations from poor widows, that paid the bill. It would be one thing if a rich businessman said, "Wherever you travel, I want you to stay in the best hotel, and I'm going to pay for it." It's another thing when most of the funds come from average ministry donors.

A close friend of mine is a worship leader, and he was shocked by what he saw firsthand while serving at a prosperous church in the States. A well-known teacher ministered at the church one Sunday, after which this leader and his wife, along with the pastor and his wife, went to an upscale mall together with my friend. In front of his eyes, they bought Rolex watches for each other, charging the bill to their respective ministries, justifying the purchases as some kind of ministry expense. What would Paul say about this?

Another colleague of mine shared a disturbing story involving one of his friends, a pastor in Canada. This pastor had invited another famous American preacher, this time a woman, to lead a series of special meetings in his city. She agreed to come and speak, but once he began to work out the details with her, he was shocked by her demands. She insisted on staying in the presidential suite at the most expensive hotel in the city, and she insisted on hiring her own audio people to run the event, all at exorbitant prices.

Because he had already announced the meetings, he felt he could not back out, so he went ahead with them anyway. (Obviously that was a big mistake.) He took a massive financial loss on the conference, but to add insult to injury, the speaker was so pleased with the way things went that she extended the meeting one more day, again at his expense. When the conference was over, this pastor, who did not have a large church, was roughly $150,000 in debt. He spent more than a year digging out of the financial hole she dug for him. This is inexcusable and unjustifiable.

But she is not the only prima donna preacher out there. Pastors have told me about the list of demands that some speakers send to them, including that they must be picked up at the airport by a limo, and in the limo there must be chilled water waiting for them (with lemon or lime or whatever), along with very specific snacks, prepared in a specific way (remember, this is just for the limo ride to the hotel); they must have twenty-four-hour chauffeur service available to them while there in case they need anything day or night; they must have a hair stylist; they will only stay at certain hotels—and this is aside from their speaking fee. Who do they think they are?

Some of my ministry colleagues are quite well known, and they appreciate it when their hosts take good care of them. As one who has traveled the world for decades preaching the gospel, I appreciate this too. But for heaven's sake, this superstar, prima donna mentality is as far from true apostleship (or true ministry leadership) as night is from day. What in the world has gotten into us? Yes, the laborer is worthy of his hire, but we are servants of the

Lord, not rock stars or movie stars, and our ministries are non-profit rather than for personal gain.

Paul exhorted Timothy to "share in suffering as a good soldier of Christ Jesus" (2 Tim. 2:3, ESV). I'm quite sure Paul would not have included getting picked up in a regular car, not a limo, as suffering for Jesus. If he were writing today, he'd have to say, "Timothy, don't throw in the towel! I know your private plane needs maintenance and your Porsche is in the shop. But hold your head high! Your next mega-offering at your next mega-meeting will put that smile back on your face."

Am I exaggerating? Not by that much.

And why must we have such large entourages with us when we travel? Do we think we're like the president of the United States, requiring a security team, a press team, several personal assistants, and perhaps our own chef? Some of the world's most famous athletes and celebrities travel with far less staff and support than some of our superstar church leaders.

Please don't tell me I don't understand the pressure these leaders are under. I know what a grueling schedule feels like, and I know what it's like to be a public figure. More to the point, I'm on several most-hated lists, and I receive regular death wishes and occasional death threats. I've spoken on college campuses where the school required us to have armed policemen present, and I've been in life-threatening situations while preaching overseas. I do understand the need for security and safety. But really, now, do we need to show up at a church conference in the United States with a big entourage? Do we even need one at all?

I read an article claiming that actor Johnny Depp spent $30,000 per month on wine and—get this—$300,000 per month on his forty-person staff.[1] Some of our superstar leaders are closer to this model than to the model of a tribal pastor in India who can be supported for $50 per month.[2] If you really wanted to bless a pastor like this, you could buy him an extra pair of trousers and a new shirt, or better still, a bicycle so he could cover more ground.

While I was speaking at a church in Seattle, Washington, about twenty years ago, the pastor told me about a bad experience he had with another American preacher. This pastor was opening a new building that seated three thousand people, and he invited a well-known speaker, who was also a pastor, to preach at the dedication. What would this preacher require? His speaking fee for a single meeting was $50,000—and remember, this was close to twenty years ago. The Seattle pastor, in shock, declined, although the guest speaker claimed that his fee was justifiable, since he would pack the building out, and as a result, the church could receive a large offering that night, thereby providing the means to put the money in his pocket.

The View From India

I made my first trip to India in 1993 and have been back twenty-five times as of 2017. In the main city where I spoke, I was told the pastors were pleased to meet an American "who preached the gospel," having had some bad experiences with other Americans who previously ministered there. They were particularly upset with the most recent, high-profile American preacher who traveled to their city.

While speaking there, this pastor from the States boasted about his $3,000 custom-made shoes. (This was at a time when the average laborer in India made one dollar a day for backbreaking work in the sun. So it would take them more than nine and a half years, working six days a week, to buy those shoes.) He also informed the Indian believers, "I tell my church members, 'If you want to see my faith, look in the parking lot at my Rolls-Royce.'" Seriously?

One of the Indian pastors said to me, "He never once talked

about the blood of Jesus in all his preaching, and because he's a rich American, he thinks he can come here and talk down to us about faith. We know about faith."

This Indian pastor had been stoned for preaching the gospel. By faith he was training, sending, and supporting church planters in primitive tribal regions. By faith he was housing, clothing, feeding, and educating orphans—just to mention some of what his ministry was doing. And he did it all without any guaranteed support from the West. Needless to say, he was not impressed with the American pastor's faith.

To be honest, though, ministers buying expensive cars doesn't prove much these days, at least in the States. Today you're measured by the quality of your private jet.

Lest you think I'm upset because I don't have a private jet (trust me, it's the last thing on my mind), let me be as clear as possible. If a ministry genuinely needs a private jet for its work and God provides it, wonderful. Let those with the ministry use it for His glory. I will be the first to rejoice with them. I have colleagues whose ministries own private planes, and these leaders are highly ethical with servant hearts. Sometimes schedule demands require this, and it's actually good stewardship of the ministry's time and funds to own and maintain a jet. (Good stewardship is the operative phrase.)

Unfortunately all too often having a private jet is more of a status symbol, something fitting for a superstar leader. After all, how could an exalted man of God travel on a commercial flight? (I once saw two Christian leaders on TV talking about this very thing. How could they fly commercial with all the demonized people on the plane?)

Having flown several million miles myself, I certainly understand the challenges involved. You have to get to the airport at least an hour early, in some cases two. Your flight might be canceled or delayed, causing you to sit for hours at an airport, or, worse still, causing you to miss your next flight, which causes you to miss your speaking slot. And even when your flights are on time, you might be on a small plane, squeezed into an uncomfortable seat. Then when you land, you have to wait for your luggage, sometimes for forty-five minutes or more. On rare occasions, your luggage doesn't make it at all, so you have to run out and buy new clothes and toiletries before you speak.

Also, on a private plane you're alone with your people, whereas if you use public transportation, others might recognize you and want to talk with you: "Pastor, I need counsel. Can you talk to me while we wait for the plane? Pastor, will you pray for me? I'm in a lot of pain. Pastor, I read your book and have lots of questions. Do you mind if I pull out my list? Pastor, I wrote this amazing new song. Can I sing it for you?"

This can be very draining, and I know of one leader who would ask men from his ministry team to make sure the church bathroom was empty before he used it. This way he could at least relieve himself in private without people asking him for prayer, even in the restroom.

You might say, "It doesn't matter. Ministers are supposed to give and serve. That's what Jesus would do." But even Jesus withdrew from the crowds to lonely places to pray. (See, for example, Luke 5:16.) And unless you've been in the spotlight, ministering until you're ready to drop, only to be approached at a restaurant by a line of people wanting prayer, it's hard to imagine how taxing this is. And when things only intensify as you travel so that you're worn out from the trip before you even arrive to minister, it becomes more difficult still.

I do understand the benefits of private jets, and I do understand the difficulties of using public transportation. It's a hassle, and it can be challenging. But it's also part of life, and it costs a fraction of the cost to fly a private plane. Yet some Christian leaders feel entitled to a private jet. After all, they are special. They are apostles. They are anointed. They are fivefold ministers. They deserve superstar treatment like this, right?

About twenty years ago I was speaking at a big conference in London, and a famous American preacher spoke the first night. During his message he boasted about his faith, telling the crowd that he covered his own expenses to fly there on his private plane. (I believe he said the gas alone was $25,000.) He also described the mansion in which he lived, saying that when some workers were there recently (they were white), they were stunned to see a man like him (he was black) living in such affluence. He remarked, "When they saw a black man living in a house like that, they knew there was a God in heaven!"

When I heard this, I said to a good friend who had traveled with me, "I wonder what those workers think when they're over at another mansion in the community, one owned by a crime boss. Does that make them think that there's a devil in hell?"

As for this pastor's boasts about paying his own way, the British leader who invited him told us the rest of the story. The host ministry in England was willing to cover his normal travel expenses, but he insisted on traveling with his entourage on his private jet. When the host ministry wouldn't cover such an outrageous cost, he asked them to cover half of the expense. When they still said no, he said, "Fine, I'll pay my own way," then he boasted about it from the pulpit as if he did so out of the goodness of his own heart. And who covered the costs of his flight? It was his supporters from around the world, people who were giving to help him reach the lost. In reality, they were also giving to help him live lavishly.

Again, to be clear, I have no problem with someone being blessed. If through God's generosity and your hard work you have a beautiful home or fine car or other nice possessions, that's great. Just make sure that those things don't steal your heart or become your treasure. (See Matthew 6:19–24 and 1 Timothy 6:17–19.)

I also believe we should honor and care for God's servants, blessing them and helping to relieve them of the financial pressures of life and ministry as much as we can. When Smith Wigglesworth was asked once why he traveled first class by train, it is reported that he replied, "I'm not saving the Lord's money. I'm saving the Lord's servant."[3] That makes sense to me, and that's ultimately a wise investment of God's funds: If you're too worn out to minister, what's the use of the money you saved?

The problem, like always, is one of extremes. How far will we go to justify "saving the Lord's servant"? If we emulated the overall lifestyle of Wigglesworth, we'd be light years away from today's superstar mentality. This man of faith did not live like a man who deserved special privileges because he was anointed. The anointing brought him down to his knees.

Dangerous Pride

I was once told about a healing evangelist who was notorious for sleeping with women on his ministry team. When one of the ladies refused his advances and confronted him, he told her, "Because of the anointing on my life, God has given me special privileges." How horrific! That kind of thinking isn't just sick; it's sinful and satanic. (For the record, the anointing is nothing to boast about either. It's God's gracious, undeserved gift to us, and it's for the good of others, not for our exaltation. We deceive ourselves if we think we are God's gift to the world.)

Later in the book I devote a whole chapter to the plague of sexual immorality in our midst, so we'll leave that painful subject for now. But I will say this one thing: One of the most respected Christian leaders in the world, now with the Lord, once told me that the common denominator among some famous preachers who committed sexual sin was pride. That, he said, was the real danger, yet it is pride that is at the root of our superstar mentality.

Once before traveling to Seoul, Korea, I read the newsletter of a rising Charismatic prophet. He had just returned from Korea, and according to his newsletter, the nation had been shaken by his ministry. It was quite a write-up. The man of God from the United States rocked the whole country. When I arrived in Seoul, I asked my friends what had happened on his trip. They said to me, "He is not welcome in our country again." Their report was quite different from his!

Sadly it seems as if he had a genuine prophetic gift, and he spoke some significant words while in Korea, words that subsequently came to pass. But he had an exalted view of his importance, and his gifting was a source of pride. He also felt he deserved special treatment. This is a plague that must be stopped.

Unfortunately as the gospel spreads like holy fire throughout some parts of the world, it has also spread like wildfire, and because of that some countries have become breeding grounds for superstar leaders who have become mega-rich off their flocks. Some of this is understandable, seeing that there has been an unprecedented gospel explosion in some parts of the world that has resulted in the most rapid church expansion in history. With so much happening so fast, it's not surprising that there are serious abuses. And there are cultural factors that play into this as well, going back to the exaltation of kings and tribal leaders. Sometimes the people *want* their leaders to become rich since they see their leaders' success as their own.

But isn't it odd that some of the wealthiest pastors in the world—and I mean staggeringly wealthy—are based in some of the poorer countries of the world? Again, if God Himself has blessed them, wonderful. If a gold mine was discovered on property they owned, or if they receive no income from their church because they were led to start a prosperous business on the side, or if they inherited wealth—whatever the legitimate reason for their riches—that's fine. They just need to be wise stewards of their wealth. But if they became multimillionaires by receiving a large salary from their impoverished congregation or poor ministry supporters, that is abusive.

Again, I'm not naming names here, nor am I judging by outward appearance. Perhaps a leader draws a large salary by the directive of his board but gives 90 percent away without anyone knowing. Perhaps his congregation insists on treating him like a king because that was their cultural way of expressing appreciation. When one of my friends pastored a congregation, he told people just to call him by his first name since he didn't like to be called "Pastor." A congregant from Africa told him, "I must call you Pastor. If I do not, I'm insulting you."

Could it be the same thing with lavishing finances on leaders in poor countries? God Himself will judge. What I do know is that some ministers equate godliness with financial gain, which Paul repudiated in the strongest possible terms, as we will see in chapter 8 (note especially 1 Timothy 6:3–5).

I also know that some ministers feel they are *entitled* to special treatment, just like the CEOs of major companies. "After all," as a Christian leader once argued, "I'm the head of a big company. Why shouldn't I be adequately compensated?"

In support of this view, some would cite Paul's instruction in 1 Timothy 5, where he wrote, "Let the elders who rule well be considered worthy of double honor, especially those who labor in preaching and teaching. For the Scripture says, 'You shall not muzzle an ox when it treads out the grain,' and, 'The laborer deserves his wages'" (1 Tim. 5:17–18, ESV). But even if Paul is saying teaching elders should receive double compensation (compared with non-teaching elders), we need to remember that: 1) church elders were not salaried in the first place; 2) an elder had to be free from the love of money (1 Tim. 3:3); and 3) the Greek suggests Paul is talking about a double-honorarium, meaning a larger gift of appreciation. But once more, context is everything. We're talking about meeting someone's needs, not making him a millionaire.

There is an early church document called *The Didache*, which means "the teaching of the twelve apostles." While it most likely does not date back to them, it is one of the earliest preserved Christian writings outside the New Testament. Note this fascinating section found in chapter 11. I have emphasized the most relevant parts:

> *But concerning the apostles and prophets, act according to the decree of the Gospel. Let every apostle who comes to you be received as the Lord. But he shall not remain more than one day; or two days, if there's a need. But if he remains three days, he is a false prophet. And when the apostle goes away, let him take nothing but bread until he lodges. If he asks for money, he is a false prophet.*
>
> And every prophet who speaks in the Spirit you shall neither try nor judge; for every sin shall be forgiven, but this sin shall not be forgiven. But not every one who speaks in the Spirit is a prophet; but only if he holds the ways of the Lord. Therefore from their ways shall the false prophet and the prophet be known.
>
> And every prophet who orders a meal in the Spirit does not eat it, unless he is indeed a false prophet. And every prophet who teaches the truth, but does not do what he teaches, is a false prophet. And every prophet, proved true, working unto the mystery of the Church in the world, yet not teaching others to do what he himself

> does, shall not be judged among you, for with God he has his judgment; for so did also the ancient prophets. *But whoever says in the Spirit, Give me money, or something else, you shall not listen to him. But if he tells you to give for others' sake who are in need, let no one judge him.*[4]

When *The Didache* encourages believers to support prophets in their midst in chapter 13, it is against this backdrop:

> But every true prophet who wants to live among you is worthy of his support. So also a true teacher is himself worthy, as the workman, of his support. Every first-fruit, therefore, of the products of wine-press and threshing-floor, of oxen and of sheep, you shall take and give to the prophets, for they are your high priests. But if you have no prophet, give it to the poor. If you make a batch of dough, take the first-fruit and give according to the commandment. So also when you open a jar of wine or of oil, take the first-fruit and give it to the prophets; and of money (silver) and clothing and every possession, take the first-fruit, as it may seem good to you, and give according to the commandment.[5]

So living together among God's people, the prophet would get his food and gifts from them as he served in their midst, thereby meeting his needs. But if he used his gift to put money in his own pocket, he was to be rejected as a false prophet. I wonder what will happen when the Lord decides to judge His church over these sins today.

Although I've ministered in Africa on only two occasions, I have friends who minister there all the time; some are even married to Africans. We've had African students graduate from our school, and we've planted ministry schools in Africa as well. *I can say without hesitation that these African believers are some of the finest Christians I know anywhere in the world.* They have vibrant faith. They are full of courage and holy fire. They are unashamed of the gospel. They are people of prayer and fasting. They put many of us in the West to shame.

They too are grieved by some of the superstar mentality they have witnessed in the African Charismatic church, and they long to see that church come into its fullness. Ironically it is the incredibly rapid, God-glorifying harvest of souls in Africa that has made it a breeding ground for charlatans and predators, but that is a problem I would gladly welcome here in the States. Yes, may so many new churches be birthed and so many new souls be saved and so many new leaders be raised up that we will have a hard time discipling them all!

Charismatic journalist and author Lee Grady observed similar problems while ministering in South America, writing:

> I've just spent two weeks in South America, where the Holy Spirit is moving in unprecedented ways. Churches are growing and average Christians are sharing their faith passionately. One recent Pew Research study showed that 1 in 5 Latin Americans now identifies as an evangelical Christian—and a majority of these are Pentecostals.[6]

This is glorious, but just as in Africa, this presents problems. Grady continues:

> But this growth is not without problems. While there are certainly many healthy Christian movements in the region, other churches are suffering from a lack of trained leadership. And untrained, untested leaders often result in spiritual abuse, false doctrines and financial corruption.[7]

He now gets more specific, explaining:

> I've become more concerned lately with leaders who declare themselves "apostles" when they have no business wearing that label. I believe true apostolic leadership is needed today, but a small army of imposters is threatening to damage the work of God. It is time to heed the apostle Paul, who warned of "false apostles" and "deceitful workers" who were "disguising themselves as apostles of Christ" (2 Cor. 11:13).[8]

Notice carefully those words "a small army of imposters is threatening to damage the work of God." That's why we must expose these "imposters," lest the work of the Spirit get tarnished.

Grady then shares these practical thoughts:

> Discerning the difference between a true and false apostle is not complicated. Since Scripture clearly tells us that Paul is our apostolic model (see 1 Cor. 4:16), we can use his surrendered life as our standard. Here are six signs that a man or woman who claims apostolic leadership is actually a dangerous influence in the church. 1. A toxic "apostle" requires the title.... 2. A toxic "apostle" carries an aura of self-importance.... 3. A toxic "apostle" is inaccessible.... 4. A toxic "apostle" dominates and controls people.... 5. A toxic "apostle" refuses to work with churches outside his network.... 6. A toxic "apostle" demands financial payment.[9]

Obviously some of these judgments are matters of perception. For example, if you have a congregation of twenty thousand people, you will be inaccessible personally to a large majority of your flock. Does that mean you're a "toxic" apostle? And perhaps to you, having the title "apostle" before your name is no different from the pastor down the street having the title "pastor" or the traveling evangelist having the title "evangelist." It's merely descriptive, and you carry it with humility. And it's possible that, as you walk in the authority of the Lord, someone misjudges you and thinks you have "an aura of self-importance."

But all that being said, Grady has definitely hit the nail on the head in reminding us that apostolic leaders are called to serve, and it is Jesus alone they are called to exalt. In the words of the Master Himself, "You know that those who are considered rulers of the Gentiles lord it over them, and their great ones exercise authority over them. But it shall not be so among you. But whoever would be great among you must be your servant, and whoever would be first among you must be slave of all. For even the Son of Man came not to be served but to serve, and to give his life as a ransom for many" (Mark 10:42–45, ESV).

What's really troubling is that, without the empowerment of the people—without their sacrificial giving and without their loyalty—there would be no such thing as superstar leaders, which leads to a simple question: Why do so many of God's people allow themselves to be taken advantage of? As Paul wrote to the Corinthians, likely referring again to the superstar leaders, "You even put up with anyone who enslaves you or exploits you or takes advantage of you or puts on airs or slaps you in the face" (2 Cor. 11:20, NIV). Why do we still do this today?

We'll get into that question in the next chapter when we discuss the misuse of the verse that says, "Touch not My anointed." But let me leave you here with a powerful quote from pastor Richard Wurmbrand. He was a Jewish believer in Jesus and a Romanian Christian leader, a fearless witness for the gospel who was twice imprisoned under the Communists, spending a total of fourteen years in horrific conditions, including three years in solitary confinement. The tortures he suffered were unimaginable, and his wife, Sabina, also a Jewish believer, suffered greatly while enslaved in a slave labor camp.[10]

Pastor Wurmbrand once told me his book *Tortured for Christ* was one of the most translated books of the twentieth century. And the ministry he founded, The Voice of the Martyrs, continues to bear great fruit to this day. I had the distinct privilege of spending a few hours with him and Sabina in private settings on two occasions, and they were almost like people from another world. They glowed with the love of Jesus, and they were powerfully marked by their sufferings for the gospel.

Pastor Wurmbrand related that before the Iron Curtain fell, the Christians who came from the States to minister there were of the highest quality, putting themselves at risk for the good of the Romanian Church. But after the Iron Curtain fell, his country was flooded with American preachers who were ready to impart their wisdom to the pastors there. Pastor Wurmbrand said, "All of these American leaders came to our country to teach our pastors, but none of them said to themselves, 'I wonder what a pastor could teach me who was chained and tortured for twenty years and never denied Jesus.'"[11]

This lies at the root of our superstar mentality: we think too highly of ourselves. Let us, then, humble ourselves before the Lord and say, "Father, I'm here to serve, not to be served, to give, not to get. Help me follow in the footsteps of Your Son." If it was good enough for Paul, it should be good enough for us.

Chapter Five
Abusive Leadership

In all settings, both secular and religious, Charismatic and non-Charismatic, leaders can be abusive, taking advantage of their people and using them for all kinds of fleshly purposes, from financial gain to sex to control. But we Charismatics can be especially prone to abusive leadership. After all, we do believe in "the anointing," and we don't want to "touch God's anointed," to sin against the man of God who is backed by the Spirit of God. And so abusive leaders can more easily take advantage of us.

One of the passages commonly cited in this context is Psalm 105:15, where God says, "Do not touch my anointed ones; do my prophets no harm" (NIV). Have you ever heard a pastor quote this verse, threatening you with divine judgment if you dared to differ with his authority? Has a self-proclaimed prophet warned you of the dire consequences of rejecting his words, using this very text? In reality, the verse has little (or nothing) to do with church leadership, as we'll see shortly. But since we Charismatics have a healthy respect for the anointing, and since we believe prophetic ministry is still in operation today, abusive leaders can hang this verse over our heads and say, "You don't dare question the man of God!"

Again, I realize this is not just a problem in our Charismatic circles, but a crafty leader will find us especially easy to victimize. As Paul wrote to the Corinthians, who were impressed with the big-shot leaders, "For you tolerate fools gladly, seeing you yourselves are wise. For you permit it if a man brings you into bondage, if a man devours you, if a man takes from you, if a man exalts himself, or if a man strikes you on the face" (2 Cor. 11:19–20; see also chapters 3 and 4). Why are we such easy prey?

Now, I can't verify this story, but I heard it firsthand from a well-known American pastor. He said that he and his wife were new believers when they attended a gospel rally in California. According to their account, when the preacher got up to speak, he said to the crowd, "You don't need your Bibles. You have a prophet of God in your midst." The moment this couple heard this, even though they were new in the Lord, they turned to each other and said, "This isn't right. We need to get out of here." And they left immediately.

Years later they found out what happened to this man. His name was Jim Jones, and he became the leader of the Peoples Temple, which became the Jonestown cult, ending with the mass suicide of more than nine hundred of his followers in Guyana.[1] As a manipulative leader, he was able to get all those families to leave the United States and relocate to an entirely new part of the world, where he lived like a king among them, reportedly having sex with multiple women and men. He was also a communist with extreme leftist views,[2] but without the spiritual element it's unlikely that he would have been able to dominate and control people to such a radical extent.

Of course, he ended up a complete heretic, but he was originally ordained as a Disciples of Christ pastor and may have started off on the right foot.[3] (At the least, he was closer to the truth at the beginning than at the end.) Either way, whether he started right or not, I'm not putting him in the category of a misguided Charismatic leader since he was a complete apostate and a cult leader. But he shared one of the key characteristics of abusive leaders: *he drew disciples after himself rather than pointing people to Jesus and creating a sense of allegiance to God and His Word.* As Paul warned the elders of Ephesus,

> Therefore take heed to yourselves and to the entire flock, over which the Holy Spirit has made you overseers, to shepherd the church of God which He purchased with His own blood. For I know that after my departure, dreadful wolves will enter among you, not sparing the flock. Even from among you men will arise speaking perverse things, to draw the disciples away after them. Therefore watch, remembering that for three years night and day I did not cease to warn everyone with tears.
>
> —ACTS 20:28–31

These people are wolves rather than shepherds, feeding off the sheep rather than feeding the sheep, fleecing them rather than nurturing them, plundering them rather than ministering to them. Can you imagine how the Good Shepherd feels about this, since He purchased this flock with His own blood? Yet that is something abusive leaders have forgotten or ignored: *these are the Lord's sheep, not their own*. The church is God's possession, not the pastor's (or the apostle's or the evangelist's or the prophet's or the teacher's), and at the end of the day these leaders will be accountable to the Great Shepherd Himself for how they treated His flock. As a leader myself, this is a sobering thought.

Look at these strong words from the prophet Ezekiel against the faithless shepherds of ancient Israel, a metaphor referring to the kings and princes and leaders. You can hear the holy jealousy of the divine Shepherd in every verse:

> And the word of the LORD came to me, saying: Son of man, prophesy against the shepherds of Israel. Prophesy and say to those shepherds, Thus says the Lord GOD: Woe to the shepherds of Israel who feed themselves! Should not the shepherds feed the flock? You eat the fat and clothe yourself with the wool; you kill those who are fed without feeding the flock. The diseased you have not

> strengthened, nor have you healed that which was sick, nor have you bound up that which was broken, nor have you brought back that which was driven away, nor have you sought that which was lost. But with force and with cruelty you have subjugated them. They were scattered because there was no shepherd. And they became meat to all the beasts of the field and were scattered. My sheep wandered through all the mountains and upon every high hill. Indeed, My flock was scattered upon all the face of the earth, and no one searched or sought after them.
>
> —EZEKIEL 34:1–6

These are extreme examples of abusive leadership, far more severe than what most of us have experienced. But I cite this passage to remind us of just how destructive such leadership can be. *Shepherds have great power over the sheep.*

Referring to Paul's warnings in 2 Corinthians 11:19–20, cultural commentator Bill Muehlenberg cites biblical scholar Linda Belleville, who "reminds us that the church today is equally in need of hearing such teaching."[4]

In her commentary on 2 Corinthians, Belleville writes:

> We may be quick to scoff at a church like Corinth. How could a church permit itself to be browbeaten like this? What kind of wimps were they to so readily accept such leadership? But are the Corinthians really so different from some of our contemporary churches? A take-charge, strong-arm style of leadership is valued by many within evangelicalism today. Those who lead in this way typically claim to be exercising their God-given authority. Interestingly enough, though, Paul rejects this style of leadership in his own ministry ("not that we lord it over your faith," 1:24)—as do other New Testament writers (for example, see Mt 20:25-26; 1 Pet 5:3).[5]

Muehlenberg weighs in with his own observations about why the Corinthians (and we ourselves) often "suffer fools gladly." He writes:

> It is not at all loving to allow our brothers and sisters in Christ to be sold down the river by false teaching, dangerous practices, or phony theologies. We should not just put up with this. We should not just tolerate it. We should not just wink at it. It is our job to confront it, to challenge it, and to resist it.
>
> So the next time you feel welling up within you the need to not suffer fools gladly, it may just be the flesh, but it may also be the Spirit of God within you, leading you into a bit of righteous indignation. While we are to test all things—including the thoughts and feelings that spring up within us—there is a place for some holy anger over idiotic ideas, dodgy doctrines, and perilous practices.[6]

But herein lies the problem. It's one thing to test prophecies and to test preaching. But how do you test pastors and leaders? How do you recognize and run from abusive leadership without falling into rebellion and unhealthy judgmentalism?

Before I share some practical thoughts on how you can protect yourself from abusive leaders, let me give you some examples of things I've heard from trustworthy sources or witnessed with my own eyes. One pastor committed sexual sin with different women in his congregation over more than a decade, making them swear by the blood of Jesus that they wouldn't tell anyone. It was bad enough that he abused his privileged position of power by taking advantage of these women. But to have them swear by the blood of Jesus that they would tell no one—how can we even describe such hypocrisy?

Other leaders abuse their power for financial profit, telling the people they will be cursed by God if they don't tithe, laying guilt trips on them before every offering. But it's one thing to truly believe that those who don't tithe are under some kind of spiritual curse, based on Malachi 3:8–12. It's another to use that belief to coerce people into giving for your own profit. As the pastor of one of the world's most wealthy churches once said to me, "If you teach your people to tithe because you want more money for your church, God won't bless it. If you teach them to tithe because you love them and want to see them blessed, God will bless that."

But abusive leaders aren't motivated by love or by what is best for the flock. They're motivated by what's best for them, by what fills a need in their lives, by how you can advance their cause, using you as their tool rather than serving you for your good. Paul's example is the polar opposite, to the point that he had to rebuke the Corinthians for thinking they could live like royalty while he and his companions suffered for their sake. As he wrote,

> For I think that God has exhibited us, the apostles, last, as if we were sentenced to death. For we have been made a spectacle to the world, to angels and to men. We are fools for Christ's sake, but you are wise in Christ. We are weak, but you are strong. You are honorable, but we are despised. Even to this present hour we both hunger and thirst, and are poorly clothed and beaten and homeless. We labor, working with our own hands. Being reviled, we bless. Being persecuted, we endure. Being slandered, we encourage. We are made as the filth of the world, and are the refuse of all things to this day.
>
> —1 Corinthians 4:9–13

So much for apostles being big shots who feed off the flock!

A Lesson From Another Leader Who Went Astray

John Alexander Dowie (1847–1907) was a pioneer healing evangelist from Scotland and Australia who developed a massive ministry in the United States and even founded a Christian city (Zion, Illinois) before dying at the age of fifty-nine. When he left this world, his ministry was on the decline, one reason being that he had proclaimed himself to be Elijah the prophet, apparently becoming senile before his death as well.[7] Sadly he was also drawing disciples to himself.

But what makes Dowie's demise even more tragic is that earlier in life, at the height of his work, he was asked if he considered himself to be an apostle. His answer, given spontaneously, is classic:

> But I am too perfectly honest when with no mock humility I say to you, from my heart, I do not think I have reached a deep enough depth of true humility...for the high office of Apostle, such as he had reached who would say, and mean it too, "I am less than the least of all saints, and not worthy to be called an Apostle." But if my good Lord can ever get me low enough, and deep enough in self-abasement and self-effacement, to be truly what I want to be, and hope in a measure I am, "a servant of the servants of the Lord," why then I should be an Apostle by really becoming the servant of all.
>
> ...If I should be called to that office, I feel I should be called, in the depths of my heart, to die. I do not think I am afraid to die for Christ. I live for him.
>
> ...I do not know if any persons here have got a notion in their minds that Apostolic Office means a high pompous position, wearing a tiara, and swaying a scepter, if so they are entirely wrong. It means a high position

> truly, an authoritative position and power truly, but the power of one who can take the lowest place.[8]

Boy, did he nail this! Dowie did not think that he had "reached a deep enough depth of true humility…for the high office of Apostle," which meant "really becoming the servant of all." No, the apostolic office does not mean "a high pompous position, wearing a tiara, and swaying a scepter," quite a striking statement when you think of this distinguished, gray-bearded man later adorned in a robe and high-priestly hat as "Elijah the Restorer."[9] Not surprisingly, during his declining years, Dowie also took advantage of his followers' money, apparently not from an evil heart as much as from an irresponsible and unaccountable heart. Whatever the case, he failed to live up to the standards he set, ruling harshly rather than serving graciously.

Amazingly it was Dowie who also said this (and these words should be read slowly and prayerfully):

> I think some of you have got a very false conception of Power in the Church of God. Power in the Church of God is not like Power in the government of the United States, where a man climbs to the top of a pyramid of his fellows to the acme of his ambition, and there makes it fulfill his personal pride and purpose. Power in the Church of God is shown in this, that a man shall get lower and lower, and lower and lower, until he can put his very spirit, soul and body underneath the miseries and at the feet of a sin-cursed and disease-smitten humanity and live and die for it and for Him who lived and died for it. This is what I understand by Apostolic Office.[10]

Dowie certainly started much more like this, living sacrificially to bring healing and salvation to multitudes of hurting and lost people. But the fleshly areas of his life became dominant (perhaps due to overwork and lack of sleep), and his death in 1907 was seen by some as an act of divine mercy. How dangerous is that "false conception of Power"!

Jesus addressed this too when teaching His disciples, who themselves were caught up in jealousy for power: "You know that the rulers of the Gentiles lord it over them, and those who are great exercise authority over them. It shall not be so among you. Whoever would be great among you, let him serve you, and whoever would be first among you, let him be your slave, even as the Son of Man did not come to be served, but to serve and to give His life as a ransom for many" (Matt. 20:25–28).

Not long after this, Jesus washed His disciples' feet, doing the work of a lowly household slave. When He was finished, He said to them:

> Do you know what I have done to you? You call Me Teacher and Lord. You speak accurately, for so I am. If I then, your Lord and Teacher, have washed your feet, you also ought to wash one another's feet. For I have given you an example, that you should do as I have done to you. Truly, truly I say to you, a servant is not greater than his master, nor is he who is sent greater than he who sent him. If you know these things, blessed are you if you do them.
>
> —JOHN 13:12–17

Do you know what enabled Jesus to do this? Do you know why He was able to go to the cross and let the world (including Satan and demons) mock Him? It's because He was totally secure in God. As John 13 states, "Jesus, knowing that the Father had given all things into His hands and that He came from God and was going to God, rose from supper, laid aside His garments, and took a towel and wrapped Himself. After that, He poured water into a basin and began to wash the disciples' feet and to wipe them with the towel with which He was wrapped" (vv. 3–5).

Secure leaders can serve. Secure leaders can get low. Secure leaders do not need to declare their authority all the time, like a cowboy shouting out, "I'm the head honcho on this ranch!" When you're anointed and called by God, people recognize it. And over time, as you serve among them, you earn their respect as well.

In contrast, insecure leaders have to keep others down. They think, "No one can outshine me!" There's even a saying that some people would rather be number one in hell than number two in heaven. That's how fragile their egos are and how insecure, weak, and ambitious they are. Jacob (James)[11] has some strong words that relate to this too: "Who is wise and understanding among you? Let him show his works by his good life in the meekness of wisdom. But if you have bitter envying and strife in your hearts, do not boast and do not lie against the truth. This wisdom descends not from above, but is earthly, unspiritual, and devilish. For where there is envying and strife, there is confusion and every evil work" (James 3:13–16).

Are we spiritual leaders or carnal leaders, servants or superstars? Do we raise up spiritual sons and daughters who can carry the torch and even surpass us, or do we glory in being the top dog, the big man (or woman), the one who must control and suppress others and become great at their expense? One type of leadership is from above and brings life and liberty; the other type is from below and brings death and bondage. Tragically many leaders with great giftings become abusive leaders, using their anointing as a weapon, while those with fewer giftings sometimes feel the need to overcompensate for their own perceived lacks, trying even harder to be dominant.

This kind of leadership creates a series of self-confirming, vicious cycles. For example, a jealous and insecure leader who thinks everyone is out to get his job will likely suffer many church splits over the years. Why? Because his style mistreats others and his suspicions push them away, causing further distrust. And since he doesn't raise people up and give them a proper outlet for their gifts, they feel the need to go elsewhere. And when they leave, they confirm his suspicions: "I knew they were power hungry and out to get my job!" (That's not the only reason for church splits, and even fine leaders can experience them. I'm simply talking about why these splits happen more often with this type of leader.)

Leaders who constantly feel the need to announce their authority and assert their dominance will overreact to honest questions and concerns since everyone is viewed as a potential rebel. And the harder these leaders push, the more people will vote with their feet, walking away from the church. This too confirms the leader's suspicions. "I knew they couldn't be trusted!" And on and on it goes.

But in many other cases, because the leader is a compelling speaker or an incredible motivator or a powerful organizer or a skilled manipulator, his influence grows and grows as more and more people come under his sway. Before you know it, he is like a king in his court, clothed in wealth and power, all at the expense of his followers, who now experience a sense of vicarious success through him. His triumph is their triumph, his prestige their prestige, his exaltation their exaltation. But is this the Jesus way? Is this the pattern of Scripture?

To say it again: if you are truly anointed and called and you live a life worthy of respect, people will recognize it and submit to your authority (in a biblical, not abusive, way). I can attest to this from my own experience as a leader and from watching other leaders I respect. Of course, some people are just plain rebels and troublemakers, but yelling and shouting and threatening and pounding our chests won't stop them either.

What we have to remember (and I say this to my fellow leaders) is that there are strong admonitions in the Word calling for believers to submit to their spiritual elder such as, "Obey your leaders and submit to them, for they watch over your souls as those who must give an account. Let them do this with joy and not complaining, for that would not be profitable to you" (Heb. 13:17). Because of this, since the Word is already calling believers to submit to their leaders, we must not lay guilt trips on our people or batter them into submission with our authority. As Paul wrote, the authority we have is designed to build up, not tear down (2 Cor. 13:10). If we lead and serve well, when we do need to assert our authority, people will listen.

As for the "touch not my anointed" verse, let's read it in context. It is speaking of Abraham, Isaac, and Jacob and their descendants before they were established as a nation in their homeland. (See Psalm 105, beginning in verse 8.) The relevant verses read:

> When they were but a few people in number, indeed, very few, and strangers in it, when they went from one nation to another, from one kingdom to another people, He did not permit anyone to do them wrong; indeed, He reproved kings on their behalf, saying, "Do not touch my anointed ones, and do no harm to my prophets."
>
> —Psalm 105:12–15

In context, then, this is not talking about questioning what your pastor says when his teaching doesn't agree with Scripture. It's not talking about differing with some prophet's carnal fund-raising methods. It's talking about the patriarchs and their descendants wandering from nation to nation and people to people. God said, "Don't mess with them!" (See Genesis 12 and 20 for good examples.) This was in keeping with God's promise to Abram that those who blessed his seed would be blessed and those who cursed it would be cursed (Gen. 12:1–3).

Now, I don't argue that there is a broader application to the verse, which is why David wouldn't hurt Saul, the rightful king and God's anointed, even though Saul tried to kill David.[12] I certainly respect this concept and do my best not to malign God's servants, even when some of them malign me. Miriam and Aaron were rebuked for speaking evil of Moses, a man with whom the Lord spoke face to face (Num. 12:1–15). We should not speak lightly about true men and women of God who really walk with the Lord.

At the same time, I recognize that New Testament pastors are not kings, that leaders today are spiritually accountable to other leaders, and that we are to be marked by humility rather than (earthly) royalty. As Peter said so well,

> I exhort the elders who are among you, as one who is also an elder and a witness of the sufferings of Christ as well as a partaker of the glory that shall be revealed: Shepherd the flock of God that is among you, take care of them, not by constraint, but willingly, not for dishonest gain, but eagerly. Do not lord over those in your charge, but be examples to the flock. And when the chief Shepherd appears, you will receive a crown of glory that will not fade away.
>
> —1 Peter 5:1–4

(For Peter's strong words to younger leaders, read the verses that follow.)

Everyone's an Apostle These Days

There's another factor today adding to abusive leadership, and it's the idea that a disproportionate number of leaders are modern-day apostles. To be sure, I do believe in apostles today, meaning "small a" apostles as opposed to "capital A" apostles, such as Peter and John and Paul. And I believe there have been true apostles throughout church history. We just didn't give them that title. (I'm thinking of leaders such as John Wesley or Hudson Taylor or William Booth.) At the same time, I believe it's important to recognize true fivefold anointings so each leader can fulfill his or her calling in the Lord. If my primary calling is evangelist, I will not be the best local church pastor unless I get the help of other shepherds in our midst. If my primary calling is prophet, I will not fit comfortably in the role of teacher. In the same way, if I'm called to apostolic ministry—to birth new works, to be a spiritual father to other leaders, to build Jesus-centered foundations—I can feel constrained by the limited expectations of some local congregations.

So I'm thrilled to see people discover their callings and anointings, and I'm all for releasing leaders into fivefold ministry. But here too the pendulum has swung, and too many pastors now call themselves apostles, leading to a further abuse of authority. It's bad enough to differ with your pastor, but you don't dare mess with an apostle! And it's a short step from proclaiming yourself to be an apostle to thinking that you carry the same authority as the first twelve apostles. That is a very serious error.

I've also seen what I call "apostle by acquisition," referring to leaders taking over other churches or ministries, thus expanding their "network." After all, doesn't every pastor need an apostle? So if you're an independent, nondenominational church, and I claim to be an apostle, perhaps you should be submitting to me (and tithing to me). I have my sales pitch ready to go!

When I served as a leader in the Brownsville Revival, people came flocking to the services from more than 130 nations, and every week thousands of people were impacted, including hundreds of leaders. To this day, twenty years later, I regularly meet people around the world who joyfully tell me they were transformed at the revival, many wanting me to know I prayed for them or they attended my day sessions. It was a once-in-a-lifetime opportunity, and all of us were amazed that we were allowed to take part in such a sacred, world-impacting event.

One day, after teaching day sessions for leaders, a man came up to me with a big binder in his hand, the kind I used when I was a traveling salesman decades ago. He said to me, "What you're doing here is great, but I want to talk to you about doing something really big, touching a lot more people." I immediately knew what he was after and said, "So you want me to come under your apostolic network?" When he responded in the affirmative, I politely told him thanks, but no thanks.

What in the world was he thinking? We had no relationship whatsoever, I was exactly where God wanted me to be and serving with other amazing leaders (to whom I was accountable), and we were at the hub of a world missions movement, especially through our school. Yet if I'd joined his group and submitted to him, I'd be part of something really big? This is *not* what it means to be an apostle. Real apostolic men will have leaders flocking to them for counsel, oversight, and encouragement because they see the heart of a genuine spiritual father.

A colleague of mine is a truly apostolic man, recognized even by his critics for the incredible gospel work he does, and in his home country he is deeply respected. A few years ago he felt called to serve the church in another nation, spending the summer there with his wife and children. Every year he would tell me with excitement about the souls who were getting saved and how the local church was getting involved with his mission. But I was absolutely shocked when I visited there and saw what was going on.

To explain briefly, when he and his family stayed in that country a few months every year, he became part of one local church, and he was helping their people do outreach. It was a fairly affluent church, and I just assumed they were backing his work. It turns out that he and his family initially lived in one tiny room—somehow, a church member thought it would be very generous to let them live there—and the church itself was not contributing a dime to his work. He and his wife provided the food for outreach and did all the legwork themselves. In other words, the congregation had no idea they had a modern-day apostle in their midst, a leader of international stature, a true man of God.

He just started attending there, told the pastor he had a burden to reach the homeless and lost, and that was it. He never announced who he was, and he never expected special treatment. That's why I was so shocked when I saw things with my own eyes. The church had no idea whom they were hosting.

Once I realized this, I said to the congregation, "Do you have any idea who this man is? Do you know he's one of the most respected leaders in his home country? Do you know his own government honors him? Do you know he has preached to more than one million people at a time?"

After that they treated him differently, but for him it was all the same. He came to serve, not to be served. His example certainly challenges me! And his example reminds us that true apostles are not abusive. The higher in the Lord you go, the less you will take advantage of others and the less you will need to announce how powerful you are.

A Checklist to Help Identify Abusive Leaders

How, then, can you determine if you are sitting under abusive leaders? You can use this as a simple checklist:

- Do they put you under pressure (even with embarrassment or threats) if you don't unquestioningly follow their lead (or, worst of all, if you contemplate leaving)?
- Are they getting rich off your giving (especially your sacrificial giving)?
- Are they lording it over you rather than leading by example?
- Do they constantly speak about their special gifting, calling, anointing, and authority?
- Do they tell you how privileged you are to have people like them at the helm?
- Are they lone rangers, lacking accountability?
- Are they harsh, mean-spirited, short-tempered, and insulting to any whose allegiance they question?

If you answered yes to any one of these questions, you might want to pray about moving elsewhere. If you answered yes to two of these questions, you should strongly consider leaving. If you answered yes to three of these questions, I'd seriously urge you to make a change before you (and/or your family) get seriously hurt. If you answered yes to all of them, by all means run for your life.

This applies to you all the more if you're not a rebel at heart, meaning that you love godly authority and want to be a committed part of a local congregation and that you're willing to serve and submit. If that's the attitude of your heart, you need not fear the threats coming your way. Just quietly move on and submit to a shepherd who is there to strengthen the flock.

A final word to my fellow leaders: If you find your security in the Lord and walk intimately with Him, He will announce to others, "This is My son [or daughter], with whom I am pleased. Listen to what he [or she] has to say!" (See Matthew 3:17.) As you diligently follow Him, others will gladly follow you. (See 1 Corinthians 11:1 and Philippians 4:9.) The Lord Himself will be your biggest backer.

Chapter Six
Unaccountable Prophecy

It is one of the great strengths of the Charismatic movement that we have so many prophetic words. After all, it was Moses who exclaimed more than three thousand years ago, "Oh, that all the people of the Lord were prophets, and that the Lord would put His Spirit upon them!" (Num. 11:29). And it was the great promise of Joel that Peter quoted in Acts 2 at Pentecost:

> "In the last days it shall be," says God, "that I will pour out My Spirit on all flesh; your sons and your daughters shall prophesy, your young men shall see visions, and your old men shall dream dreams. Even on My menservants and maidservants I will pour out My Spirit in those days; and they shall prophesy."
>
> —Acts 2:17–18

The fact that so many people, and not just a tiny, select group of prophets, deliver prophetic words is something truly remarkable. This is one of the true signs that the Spirit has been poured out. At the same time, it is one of the great weaknesses of the Charismatic movement that we have so little accountability for all these prophetic words.

Not that long ago a fairly well-known prophet was caught borrowing a psychic's predictions, repeating her "prophecies" virtually verbatim. When he was confronted by others (thankfully, this time by other Charismatic prophets), he claimed she received the words from him. The only problem was that her predictions were released well before he gave his predictions, further exposing his error.

But this was an extreme case. The vast majority of prophetic abuses are not on this scale and are not called out by other Charismatic leaders. (For the very abusive practice of prophesying for money, which is hardly called out, see chapter 3.) All too often prophets deliver words with little or no accountability, even if they are inaccurate or never come to pass. It's as if the words are spoken into the wind and carried away, never to be quoted again unless they happen to come to pass. In that case we're reminded of those prophecies again and again. As for those that don't come pass? Well, we're told, it could be because there were conditions involved that were not met; or it could be we didn't really understand the prophecy, which was cloaked in mystical language; or it could be that it will still come to pass, only not yet, and we were off in our timing.

What makes things more difficult is that all these factors could be real. It's possible that conditions weren't met. (See Jeremiah 18:1–10.) It's possible that we misunderstood the prophecy. (Can you tell me the meaning of a prophecy like the one in Zechariah 5:5–11, where there was a woman in an ephah basket and then two women with wings like a stork's carrying the basket between heaven and earth to build a house for it in the land of Shinar?) And it's possible that we got our timing wrong. (See 1 Peter 1:10–12.) But what about all the prophecies that do not fit in this category, such as, "The Lord showed me that so-and-so will be the next president of the United States." Or, "The Lord says this will be a year of great financial prosperity for the nation"—with no condition given. And what about personal prophecies that we get wrong? Do we just say, "Hey, nobody's perfect?" Or do we try to find out why we "missed it," to use our standard term, and perhaps prophesy with more humility the next time (as in telling the person to whom we're prophesying, "I sense the Lord could be showing me this; does it bear witness with your spirit?")?

When I was a new believer, the pastor of the church I attended told a humorous story (though I'm not sure if it was true or just meant as an illustration). He said a man was prophesying over people in a church service, and he had a word for a woman: "The Lord says you are called as a missionary to China!" A little while later he had a word for a man: "The Lord says you are called as a missionary to India!"

Well, it turns out these two were a couple, and the speaker didn't know it since they were in different parts of the building when he was ministering. When they got into their car, the wife was excited to share the news with her husband: "The man of God had a word for me, and we're called to be missionaries to China!" He said, "Actually, the man of God had a word for me, and we're called to be missionaries to India!"

Perturbed, they went back into the building and found the minister, explaining their dilemma. "You told me that I'm called to India," the husband said, "but you told my wife she's called to China. How can that be?" The prophet replied, "The Lord is calling you two to Indochina!"

It may be a funny story, but stuff like this (and much worse) happens all the time. Why don't we address it?

I was once part of the leadership team overseeing a number of large stadium meetings. The day after one of the meetings we met to evaluate what took place. One of the leaders said, "Well, some prophets declared that the stadium would be full, and we were expecting that, but instead we had about thirty-five thousand in a stadium that seated ninety thousand."

The most senior leader there, respected as an apostle, responded immediately with concern. "Who were these men? There must be some accountability. What they said did not happen." I was pleased to see this, but responses like this are relatively rare.

Do we just think prophecies are inspired guesswork? That they're totally hit or miss? That we have as good a chance of speaking accurately as inaccurately? That we really can't take prophetic words too seriously? If so, then why couch them in divine language? Better to say, "I have a feeling that this is going to happen. Let's pray and see." But if we say, "The Lord says," or, "The Lord showed me," we had better be sure about our words.

Without question the New Testament calls for prophetic words to be tested, which indicates that in this era, when everyone can potentially prophesy, we cannot take everything at face value. Prophecies must be judged. (See 1 Corinthians 14:29 and 1 Thessalonians 5:19–21.) This is in contrast with the Old Testament, when the penalty for false prophecy, especially presumptuous false prophecy, was death. (See Deuteronomy 18:15–22.) That is obviously not the case today, especially when so many people can prophesy. Rather, words are to be spoken responsibly, after which others—ideally, other prophets, when possible—must weigh carefully what is said.

And Paul reminds us not to despise prophecies. It appears that in his day too there were abuses because of the profusion of the gift. Plus, sometimes prophetic words don't make a lot of sense at first, so it would be easy to dismiss them or even despise them. Paul says we dare not do that, giving us these words of wisdom: "Do not quench the Spirit. Do not despise prophecies. Examine all things. Firmly hold onto what is good" (1 Thess. 5:19–21). There's a beautiful balance described here, and it's essential that we find that balance. The reputation of the Lord is at stake, not to mention the well-being of many souls.

True Prophecy Is Life-Giving

Although I don't go looking for prophetic words, at a few key times in my life God sent leaders to me with prophetic words, and they were incredibly life-giving. During one very difficult season, when there was tremendous pressure to compromise my convictions—and in the name of the Lord at that—four different leaders came to me with prophetic words. One was from England, one from India, one from Germany, and one from the States. None of them had any idea what was going on, and all of them spoke with incredible accuracy into the situation, each from a slightly different angle. It's hard to describe what a lifesaver those words were at such a difficult time.

Many of us have also received or given words that sounded very odd, such as the "dead bird" prophecy a colleague of mine received years ago. He was praying over a woman on a prayer line when he heard the words "dead bird," and he knew he was supposed to speak them to her. But he resisted. What kind of prophecy is this? Finally he said to her, "I don't know what this means, but I heard the Lord saying to me, 'Dead bird.'" Immediately she broke down weeping, and she received a significant inner healing that night.

It turned out she lost her parents as a child and sent to live in an orphanage, with her only important possession being her little bird, which was housed in its cage. When she went to sleep that first night, she was told she couldn't keep the cage in her room and that it had to be put outside until morning. Well, it was cold outside, and in the morning the bird was dead.

That event had left a lifelong wound, one that was healed the night she received that prophetic word from my friend. And all because that leader had the sensitivity to hear the Spirit's voice and share that "dead bird" word with a hurting woman.

Here's an even more unusual account. A friend of mine was at a Bible study when a prophetic brother had a word for a young woman there. But how could he deliver it? How could he say, "The Lord says, 'I hate mommies and daddies'"? It almost sounded blasphemous.

But he knew the voice of God too well to resist, so he delivered the word to this young woman, and she began to sob, receiving a significant emotional healing in her life. It turns out that she had been sexually abused for a period of years by her father, who used to come into her room and say, "We're going to play 'mommies and daddies.'" That's what he called it when he would abuse her, and now the Lord was saying, "I was there when that happened, I saw what you suffered, and I hated it too." What a prophetic message!

One of my friends served as an administrator for a major ministry, and as far as I knew, his role was behind the scenes, serving other leaders. A well-known prophetess had a word for him one day that was totally out of the blue. He needed three new suits because he was going to be meeting with government leaders. (Before that time I had never once seen him dressed up. He was always dressed casually in jeans.) Shortly after that prophetic word, also quite out of the blue, someone bought him three new suits completely unsolicited. Not long after that he was meeting with governors and congressmen and other political leaders, even working directly for some presidential candidates.

Another prophetess was scheduled to speak at a special church dinner, and the Lord laid on her heart that she would have a prophetic word for everyone there. Was this realistic? When she arrived at the building, there was a table in the front of the room with about ten people sitting there. No problem to minister to each of them! But then the doors swung open, and there were hundreds of people there. How could she possibly have a word for everyone there?

At that moment her eyes fell on an elderly woman sitting at that front table, and this prophetess heard the Lord say, "Tell her, the Lord says, 'Keep on truckin'!'" Yes, that was the word she heard, but she struggled to deliver it. How does she tell an elderly woman at a dinner that the Lord says to her, "Keep on truckin'!" But she knew His voice and delivered the message, and immediately the whole place erupted in shouts and praise and laughter.

It turns out that this woman's husband had recently died, and he owned a big trucking company. The whole church was praying for her, asking the Lord if she should keep the trucking business going, and here the Lord sends a prophetess with the message, "The Lord says, 'Keep on truckin'!'" That was the word for everyone there, and it was as genuine and heaven-breathed as they come.

Recently my physical trainer, who is also a gifted evangelist, was ministering at a church and felt prompted to ask one particular woman if she had tried to bring someone else to the meeting that night. She said she had reached out to an unsaved friend of hers, asking her to come along, but the friend didn't make it. He said to her, "Text her right now, and ask her if the words *my bella vita* mean anything to her." The woman texted her and, to her shock, received this immediate response: "I have those words tattooed on my arm!" The next night she was there and gave her life to the Lord. What a word from heaven!

I could go on and on with examples such as these, including other amazing prophetic words I've received from the Lord. And you may be able to add your own examples as well. But I give these examples to make perfectly clear that *I am not denigrating prophetic words.* To the contrary, I have the utmost respect for these Spirit-inspired utterances, and I'm jealous to see prophecy used to the full. And that means we need to do a better job of separating the wheat from the chaff, lest a multitude of inaccurate words obscure the true ones.

Look at what Paul writes in 1 Corinthians 14: "Let two or three prophets speak, and let the others judge. If anything is revealed to another that sits by, let the first keep silent. For you may all prophesy one by one, that all may learn and all may be encouraged. The spirits of the prophets are subject to the prophets. For God is not the author of confusion, but of peace, as in all churches of the saints" (vv. 29–33).

So there is order, and there is accountability. But there is also impact: if everyone is prophesying and someone comes into your service who is not a believer or who is spiritually ignorant, "he is convinced by all and judged by all. Thus the secrets of his heart are revealed. And so falling down on his face, he will worship God and report that God is truly among you" (1 Cor. 14:24–25).

One of my friends shared the story of a nonbelieving gay man who attended one of his church services. Several prophetic words came forward, focusing on the depth of God's love and speaking with real specificity about wounding and hurt. In a moment this unsaved visitor was reduced to sobbing and weeping, as the Spirit spoke right to him, convicting him of his sin and pointing him to the Lord for salvation. He was born again that day. That is the power of prophecy, and we need to see it fully operative today. Yet when so many inaccurate, unaccountable words are spoken, we cheapen the exercise of the gift.

I remember hearing words from a major TV minister about the angel of the Lord touching down in a particular city to bring revival that year. Nothing ever came of it, and I doubt anyone in leadership ever dealt with it. It was just another missed prophecy.

I've read articles summarizing words for the coming year put together by a gathering of prophets, and many (sometimes most) of them didn't come to pass. Was there any accountability, any soul searching, any seeking of God with a humble heart?

The challenge here is to do what Paul said to the Thessalonians in 1 Thessalonians 5:19–21: First, we must be careful not to put out the Spirit's fire. We don't want to become skeptical, cynical, or unbelieving. Second, we must not develop a negative attitude toward prophetic words. Third, we must test everything by the Word and by the Spirit and pay attention to whether a word was given at the right time and if it proved to be accurate. Fourth, we must hold on to the good. Are we willing to go through the process?

Remember what Paul exhorted the Corinthians: "Follow after love and desire spiritual gifts, but especially that you may prophesy....Eagerly desire to prophesy" (1 Cor. 14:1, 39). This is an important gift, and it needs to be cultivated in our midst—not snuffed out so that we hardly prophesy anymore and not left to grow like a weed, without any checks or balances. Instead, because of its importance prophecy is a gift for us to cherish. We honor the gift, we examine the gift, and we hold fast to the real gift. This is the Spirit speaking to us!

In the 1980s a prophet came to the school where I was teaching and ministered to the students. He had some very accurate words but also some words that were way off, including one where he was zero for three. Specifically he called out one young lady and said three things to her: the Lord was healing her back, He heard the prayer she had prayed early on Thursday morning, and God was going to resolve that family conflict she was dealing with. He then asked her, "Does that mean anything to you?" She answered, with respect, "My back is fine, I wasn't praying Thursday morning, and I'm not having any family conflict."

He turned to the director of the school and said, "Brother, they'll understand this more as they grow in the Lord." Then he continued to minister, without skipping a beat. As far as I know, he ministered for decades after that and was very popular, delivering some amazing words over the years. I imagine he also had quite a few clinkers along the way. Again, I ask: Was there any accountability? Were there any leaders who spoke into his life? Did he engage in self-examination before the Lord?

I'm sure the people who were blessed by his ministry can point to his many fine qualities, and I don't deny those at all. But how about those who were hurt by false words? Shouldn't we care about them too? How many times have we prophesied that a sick person will not die, yet he did? How many times have we assured someone that deliverance will come, and it didn't? Do we simply march on with a shrug of our shoulders, or do we get on our faces before the Lord and ask, "How did I get this wrong? What did I miss?"

To ask again, is there any accountability for our words? Practically speaking, how are we living out Paul's guidelines for testing and judging? If some of us pruned our prophetic tree, to use a gardening idiom, cutting back on the volume of words we deliver, what we speak would be much more accurate.

Practicing What I Preach

In 1988 I was scheduled to minister at a major conference in Israel. The organizers believed it would be the largest gathering of Messianic Jews in Jerusalem since the first century, and it was going to be held on Pentecost (Shavuot) on the fortieth anniversary of Israel. Talk about a divine setup! And I was invited to bring one of the three keynote messages.

I sought the Lord earnestly, going on a twenty-one-day water fast (the longest of my life), crying out for God's glory and for an outpouring in Israel, and the Lord gripped me with a message for the conference. The fire was going to fall! As we rode the bus from the airport to the hotel, I saw charred ground everywhere, the result of terrible forest fires that had plagued the country that year. Immediately I said to myself, "First the natural fire, then the spiritual fire."

Once we arrived at the conference, I was disappointed with some of the messages, feeling they were just designed to put pressure on the Jewish attendees to move to Israel. And I felt some of the other messages were superficial, surely not as important as the message that was on my heart.

The day I was scheduled to preach, I spent the entire day in prayer, seeking God for that night's meeting. And I was wrestling with a question: I felt the Lord showed me we would have a great outpouring that night, with visible signs of the Spirit's working, but I wasn't sure if I should say anything in advance. Part of me (the wiser part) said, "Don't announce the details in advance. It will seem like manipulation." Another part of me (the less wise part) said, "You need to announce things specifically to build the people's expectation and faith."

When the moment finally arrived for me to preach, I preached with passion, and I really believe the overall message was from the Lord. I also said that *if* we came together in hunger before the Lord, He would pour out His Spirit mightily, listing the things I expected to see happen. And then we had an altar call and sought the Lord for several hours, ending the meeting around 3:00 a.m.

On the positive side, one local Israeli believer told me it was the greatest outpouring in the history of modern Israel, while others told me of the increased liberty they felt sharing the gospel on the streets in the days that followed. And over the years attendees from that conference told me that the very things I said would happen did take place. In fact, in late 2017 one of the most respected leaders in Israel told me that from that night on things have been different among believers in the land. So, technically speaking, what I spoke came to pass. Plus, everything I said was conditional on our coming together in hunger for the Lord.

But I do not want to paint a false picture here. Many people (including my wife, Nancy, and some of my closest friends) were disappointed, feeling the picture I painted in advance was not accurate. And there is no question that my conditional "if" was not nearly as loud as my proclamation of what would happen. Others who were there through the night also believed my words were not accurate. To make matters worse, there was some division among the believers there, with one group actually opposing me as I spoke. (I only learned about this afterward.) They were all too happy to say that I overhyped what was going to happen at the meeting.

The whole experience was devastating for me, and I sought the Lord about it for months. Why did I make such a big mistake on such an important platform? Why didn't I act wisely, since I knew that was the right way to go? I discussed the event in depth with my leadership team, I put a moratorium on bringing prophetic words until I could understand why I blew it that night, and then I wrote a letter of apology to the other leaders in attendance, asking forgiveness for any confusion I caused.

After five months of much prayer and earnest seeking of God, I received some important answers, including the fact that God brought me to Jerusalem to kill some fleshly pride in me. Most importantly he showed me that I wrongly judged others, as if my message were more important than theirs, as if I were anointed more than them. (Here's an important word to all leaders and ministers: There is only one Savior, and His name is Jesus. We are just servants.) It's not so much that I over-exalted myself. Instead, I under-appreciated others.

Almost two years later I listened to the message again and wept, feeling that I sounded proud when introducing the sermon that night, describing how I had fasted for three weeks and prayed all day in preparation for the message. (No one had accused me of sounding proud; this was just the Spirit convicting me.) And in response to a prophetic word from a friend, I wrote a second letter of apology, this one much deeper. Amazingly the Lord used that letter to start a process of reconciliation between the two main Messianic Jewish groups that had been divided for years, as one leader after another wrote a humble apology to the other group, and the results were glorious. And for many years now I have had the joy of ministering for the group that most strongly criticized me that night.

So yes, I do take prophetic accountability very seriously, and in calling for it here, I am practicing what I preach.

Going Beyond Skin Deep

Some decades back, there seemed to be a wave of personal prophecies, with more and more prophetic leaders ministering individual words. Some of these prophets came to my hometown, and I attended a special leadership gathering where they taught and then prayed over us, giving each of us prophetic words. What was spoken over me and over my wife, Nancy, was quite accurate, and it was obvious they were being used by the Lord. But it was also striking that virtually every pastor there received a word of mega-blessing, with promises of supernatural growth in their congregations—and I mean megachurch type of growth.

Afterward my friends and I wondered about this. Why were all the words so incredibly positive? Why in no circumstance was there a need to take someone aside in private and bring a word of correction? Why was everyone destined to be a megachurch pastor, including one leader who we knew had been in and out of sin?

When I got home from the meeting, the Lord stirred my heart

in prayer, and I believe He gave me this word. Please do test it before our Father.

> "I want prophets," says the LORD, "who will know My heart and not just My voice, My ways and not just My words, My pain and not just My power. I *want*," says the LORD, "prophets."
>
> "But where are the Elijahs of *God*?" says the God of Elijah. "Where are *My* men? Where are the *intercessors* who *hear* and speak?" says the LORD. "The prophets who moan and weep? Everybody is running," says the LORD, "everybody is running—but I have not sent them all. Everybody has a message," says the LORD, "everybody has their pet. But *I* have a burden," says the LORD, "and *I* have a word. And *My* word pulls down powers of darkness, and *My* word consumes. *My* word is full of My life, and *My* word heals. *My* Word," says the LORD.
>
> "For there are prophets, and there are prophets," says the LORD, "and I called men prophets in My Word who were not even prophets at all. [For those who bring oracles in My name are called prophets.] Now if these men who were not even prophets were called prophets, don't let it disturb you if I call men prophets today who are only partially prophets."

Could it be that there is a deeper dimension of prophetic ministry to which the Lord is calling us? Could it be that it's not just a matter of delivering machine gun prophecies, one after another, to an endless line of recipients? Could it be there's also a brokenhearted dimension to prophecy, one that feels God's pain and calls His people to share it with Him? Are prophecies like that off-limits? Could it be that He wants to speak some words that will arrest the hearts of His people nationwide, bringing us to repentance before Him? Why must everything be upbeat, easy, and happy?[1]

Could it also be that so many of us are seeking the wrong thing when we go around looking for prophetic words? Don't we have an intimate relationship with the Lord and *fellowship* with His Spirit? (See 2 Corinthians 13:14.) Didn't Jesus say that His sheep—that means you and me—hear His voice and follow Him? (See John 10:27.) Aren't we beloved children of the Father who have access to His throne of grace day and night? (See Hebrews 4:14–16.) Why, then, are we searching for prophetic words?

It was also in the late 1980s that one of my friends started attending prophetic conferences, purchasing a "prophetic notebook" and writing down the words he received. One word was very long—I think the minister prophesied to him for close to thirty minutes—and he told me it would take many years to see if the words spoken were true. At one point I became burdened for him, seeking the Lord in prayer on his behalf. I felt the Lord gave me a word for him, and I asked him if I could share it. He welcomed it gladly, and I said this: "The Lord says, 'No more words!'" He received it with a smile and stopped chasing prophecies.

Perhaps the Lord is speaking that same word to some of us today. Perhaps if we stopped chasing prophetic words, we'd receive fewer incorrect words. And how about chasing *the Word*—as in the Bible—the way we chase after some prophets? Wouldn't *that* be a life changer!

Why Must the Critics Do the Correcting?

Because I live in the worlds of apologetics, biblical scholarship, and the culture wars *along with* the Charismatic-Pentecostal world, many people who follow my ministry are not themselves Charismatic. They don't believe the gifts of the Spirit are for today.

In fact, they think I'm very wrong in these beliefs, but they love me and appreciate my work in these other areas. Still, they are baffled when they see so many unchecked, uncorrected abuses in our midst, and in response some of them become downright hostile.

Without a doubt these critics are throwing out the baby with the bathwater, and without a doubt their attacks are sometimes more harmful than helpful.[2] But why must the critics take the initiative in bringing correction? Wouldn't it be better if we cleaned house ourselves? Wouldn't it be better if the criticism was constructive rather than destructive, designed to build up rather than tear down?

There's a biblical principle that basically goes like this: if we don't judge ourselves, others will judge us—and their judgment will be far costlier than our own. So what will it be? Will we rightly esteem the precious gift of prophecy, removing the dross from the silver and the worthless from the worthy? If we take the gift more seriously, God will speak to us more powerfully. It's time for some prophetic accountability. Let it start with you and with me. And let it be for the glory of the Lord. Why should He get discredited because of our spiritual laziness? Why should a powerful movement be maligned because of our sloppiness? It's time to show Him honor.

Chapter Seven
Sexual Immorality

Sexual sin has deadly consequences, and adultery is the ultimate act of betrayal. That's why in the Old Testament when God wanted to portray Israel's apostasy, He spoke of Israel as an unfaithful bride who committed adultery against Him. How this wounded the heart of God! Israel played the harlot, sleeping with many lovers (meaning it worshipped other gods), virtually spitting in the face of the Lord.[1]

This is a powerful spiritual picture, and it is one we can relate to all too well. That's why the Lord used adultery as a metaphor for idolatry—it's the sin of stealing the love that belongs to our Redeemer and giving it to others who do not deserve it. That's just one of the reasons we must flee from sexual immorality as if our lives depend on it. It is a terribly destructive sin and one that we can easily fall into.

Look at Paul's words to the Corinthians. He could not have been plainer:

> Now the body is not for sexual immorality, but for the Lord, and the Lord is for the body. God has raised up the Lord and will also raise us up by His own power. Do you not know that your bodies are the parts of Christ? Shall I then take the parts of Christ and make them the parts of a harlot? God forbid! What? Do you not know that he who is joined to a harlot is one body with her? For "the two," He says, "shall become one flesh." But he who is joined to the Lord becomes one spirit with Him.
>
> —1 Corinthians 6:13–17

We are made for the Lord, not for sexual immorality, and since we have been joined to the Lord, if we join our bodies to a prostitute, we are joining the body of Christ to a harlot. God forbid!

Paul continues:

> Flee sexual immorality! "Every sin a person commits is outside of the body"—but the immoral person sins against his own body. Or do you not know that your body is the temple of the Holy Spirit who is in you, whom you have from God, and you are not your own? For you were bought at a price. Therefore glorify God with your body.
>
> —1 Corinthians 6:18–20, NET Bible

How tragic that we have fallen so far short here. This deeply grieves the Lord, and it deeply hurts His people. It also hurts the people of the world since our sexual sin makes Jesus look bad, thereby driving the lost away from their Savior rather than toward Him.

I knew a pastor who was an incredible soul winner, responsible for personally leading the majority of his congregation to the Lord. With sadness he told me what happened in his city, which was the same city in which a very famous preacher was based. This preacher was exposed for sexual sin, and the pastor explained to me that after his fall it became more difficult to share the gospel with the lost. But because the fallen leader made a strong showing of public repentance, the damage was minimized.

Then, a few years later, this same preacher was caught in sexual sin again, after which time the pastor told me it was all but impossible to talk to the lost about Jesus. The moment he would bring up the gospel, people would say to him, "Oh yeah, that's what that preacher believed."

What horrific consequences! I doubt this leader ever thought to himself, "If I commit this sexual sin, I'll be driving millions of people away from Jesus." Instead, he was probably living a self-deceived double life. *It can happen to any of us if we are not careful.*

So when it comes to leaders falling into sin, the last thing I want to do is heap further condemnation on their heads. I believe in showing mercy, I live by the kindness of God 24/7, and I'm all for restoration, knowing that our God is a redeemer. I'm also the last one to throw stones at my fallen brothers and sisters, knowing full well that "there go I but for the grace of God." I could have messed up just like these others, and my trust is in the Lord's keeping power, not the strength of my will. He knows that I am broken, not boastful, always mindful of Paul's warning: "Therefore let him who thinks he stands take heed, lest he fall" (1 Cor. 10:12). I assure you that every word in this chapter was written in the fear of the Lord.

I'm also quite aware that sexual sin is rampant among non-Charismatics too, and if Solomon could be seduced by it, any of us could be. (See Nehemiah 13:26.) That's why Paul wrote about it with such passion, and that's why he always put sexual sin first in his list of sins of the flesh.[2] Sexual sin is as ugly as it is deadly, while sexual purity is as beautiful as it is healthy. That's why all of us must be on guard against immorality, whether or not we're Charismatics.

Still, there seems to be a disproportionate amount of sexual sin in our Charismatic circles, to the point that we're somewhat infamous for our scandals. This is especially tragic when you realize that the modern Pentecostal movement came out of strong holiness traditions and that we claim to be the people of the Holy Spirit (and note carefully the word *holy*). Sadly *we do not have a reputation for holiness*. In fact, we're often known for looseness more than holiness and for license more than purity. Surely this dishonors the Spirit.

In Corinth, Paul dealt with an unrepentant man who was sleeping with his father's wife, and he instructed the believers there to deal with him in the strongest terms. But from all we know, the man was not an elder or congregational leader.[3] Today, we've had to deal with far worse situations, such as a megachurch pastor who slept with his brother's wife and fathered a child by her. Years later that child, who thought he was the megachurch pastor's nephew, took his place as the new pastor of the church, only to find out that his "uncle" was his father. So the leadership succession in this congregation went from the father to the son born out of adultery and incest.[4]

I once heard reports that some guest speakers at this church were offered their pick of women to sleep with, but I dismissed the accounts as absurd. Once this scandal came to light, I wondered if these other stories were true as well. God help us.

One leader told me about a famous preacher whose limo driver would take him into the inner city after he spoke so he could pick up teenage boys. I heard about another leader who was outed by his brother after pressuring women to give him oral sex. And how many ministers do we know of who committed adultery, divorced their wives, married the women they were having an affair with, and continued with their ministries?

Again, I believe in redemption, and it's true that David married Bathsheba after committing adultery with her and then killing her husband, Uriah. It's also true that Solomon was born of their union, and he was greatly blessed by God. It's even true that Bathsheba became part of the genealogy of Jesus. (See Matthew 1:6.) But David also repented deeply (Psalm 51); the child conceived in adultery died as a baby; Solomon ended up being a terrible womanizer, leading to his apostasy; and David's reign was not the same after his sin. That's why even though we honor David today—for many good reasons—and we sing and read the psalms he wrote, his adultery and murder are part of his résumé. As it is written in 1 Kings 15:5, "David did that which was right in the eyes of the Lord and did not turn aside from anything that He commanded him all the days of his life, except in the matter involving Uriah the Hittite."

Years ago a close friend of mine committed adultery, showing few signs of true remorse when he was caught. But one of his respected colleagues advised me against seeking to remove him from ministry—even for a season of restoration—telling me that the worst thing he could do was stop preaching. After all, he was still anointed and called, right? Why remove him for skipping town with another woman? Why remove him for returning from his fling and boasting to his church about the moves he made in bed? Yet this respected leader said it would be wrongheaded to make him step down, even with a plan for counseling and a potential return to ministry in place. What kind of thinking is this?

Again, I realize sexual sin is rampant today in both non-Charismatic and Charismatic circles, and everyone has more access to sexually explicit material than any generation in history—by far. The most hardcore images, videos, and chat rooms are just a click away, and even young children are viewing porn. But that's why we need to be more vigilant. And that's why we can't make excuses for sexual sin, especially those of us who are leaders. We must face up to the problem, we must acknowledge the problem, and we must work together with the Lord and with one another to provide antidotes to the problem.

Candidly I don't think we have recovered from the mid- to late 1980s, when two of the most prominent Charismatic leaders, both with massive TV ministries, were caught in sin. When the first leader went down, I was saddened but not totally surprised, since I was never comfortable with his TV show. But when the second leader went down, I was shocked, since he was an uncompromising holiness preacher. Not him! Not the guy who railed against sexual sin from the pulpit while waving his Bible overhead! Perhaps he was a little bit too harsh, and perhaps he shouldn't have mocked the first TV minister who fell. But for him to be in sexual sin too? How could this be?

When a friend told me he had been caught in immorality, I said, "It can't be true!" But when the reality sunk in, I was overwhelmed with a sense of *corporate* sin, that his sin was *our* sin: He was a representative picture of the American church, especially the Charismatic church. His fall was our fall. I grieved and searched my own heart, praying for him as well as for myself. It was certainly a dark day for the body.

Since then Americans have been much more skeptical of what they call "televangelists," associating TV preachers with con men who are in it for the money, not to mention probably fooling around on the side. This is a shameful situation, and again I say this with brokenness, not with self-righteousness.

Paul urged *all believers* to "be blameless and harmless, sons of God, without fault, in the midst of a crooked and perverse generation, in which you shine as lights in the world" (Phil. 2:15). As for elders and overseers, he wrote that they "must be blameless, the husband of one wife, sober, self-controlled, respectable, hospitable, able to teach; not given to drunkenness, not violent, not greedy for money, but patient, not argumentative, not covetous; and one who manages his own house well, having his children in submission with all reverence" (1 Tim. 3:2–4). Also, "he must have a good reputation among those who are outsiders, so that he does not fall into reproach and the snare of the devil" (1 Tim. 3:7). Being in leadership is serious business before God and man.

Why Is Sexual Sin So Prevalent?

It's true that there have always been charlatans, and in America, a movie about a corrupt preacher, *Elmer Gantry*, was a big hit decades ago.[5] But there's no question that scandals of all kinds are much more common today, especially sexual scandals. This is a destructive plague that must be uprooted by the grace and truth of God.

Why, then, is sexual sin so prevalent in our midst? Here are some of the most obvious reasons.

Idolatry

Throughout the Bible where you find idolatry, you find immorality,[6] and the ultimate idolatry is the idolatry of *me*. It's the mentality that says, "The world revolves around me. I draw attention to myself. I am an object of people's worship and adoration. God may be important, but so am I."

Certainly this sounds extreme, but when you are hailed as the anointed man of God, when multitudes hang on your every word, when you are more of a superstar than a servant, when your name becomes more prominent than the name of Jesus, idolatry is near. And with idolatry there is immorality.

In the early 1970s a pastor on the East Coast experienced a spiritual outpouring in his church. Soon he was drawing crowds from the neighboring towns and many were being saved. He decided to rent a big coliseum that seated twenty thousand people. Posters were made advertising these "heaven on earth" meetings. Jesus, pictured as prominent and powerful, stood exalted over the coliseum. A little picture of the pastor appeared below. And when the meetings were held, the coliseum was filled. It appeared to be a great success.

A leading ministry out West heard about this pastor and began to counsel him. They told him to name his daily radio broadcast after himself instead of using the church name, and they gave him advertising suggestions, which he followed to a tee. As a result, the second year, the advertising posters had a great big picture of the pastor standing over the coliseum, with a little Jesus standing below. The third year Jesus was nowhere to be found on the posters. (Come to think of it, by that point Jesus may not have minded being left out!) I saw all this with my own eyes. His ministry even sent out a little pendant you could wear, inscribed with the pastor's face.[7] Is this not idolatry?

I once asked a pastoral couple about a leader they supported since I was troubled by his ministry's logo, which featured a globe with a banner wrapped around it that had the leader's name on it. I asked them, "Shouldn't he be promoting the name of Jesus? It's one thing to have his name in his ministry, but to have his name on a banner circling the globe—isn't that a bit much?"

The couple explained his philosophy to me. "He feels that everyone has heard about Jesus," they said, "but the world has a wrong view of Him. The solution, then, is to get the whole world to know *this minister's name*, then he in turn will tell the world about the real Jesus."

While I'm all for using our platforms to make Jesus known—the bigger the platform, the better—this leader's line of reasoning was a bit suspicious to me. Can you imagine working so hard to promote *your own name*?

This idolatrous exaltation of self produces a deadly spiritual mixture, one that is rife with deception and seduction and one that is fertile breeding ground for immorality. Superstar preachers deserve superstar treatment, right? And that includes some special perks too, like maybe an affair or two on the side. If the words of Paul that I quoted earlier were ever relevant, they are for famous leaders: "Therefore let him who thinks he stands take heed, lest he fall" (1 Cor. 10:12).

Power

We Charismatics know a lot about power—and I mean the power of the Spirit. We have seen God perform miracles through us and have felt His anointing flowing through our bodies. We have touched sick people with our hands and seen sickness and disease leave on the spot. We have watched people fall to the ground because of the Spirit's presence in our lives, and crowds have surrounded our vehicles as we drove away. This can be very humbling, as you realize you are nothing and He is everything. But it can also be very self-inflating, since you think to yourself, "Power is flowing through me."

In the 1980s I was given the nickname "Knock-'em-down Brown" because people were "slain in the Spirit" when I prayed for them. But when I served in the Brownsville Revival from 1996–2000, things intensified greatly. I watched men much bigger than me—and I'm almost six feet three inches—fly through the air as if hit by a bomb the moment I laid hands on them (actually, sometimes barely touching them with one finger). And I have seen them fall to the floor weeping and shaking, even though ten seconds earlier they were mocking. That is power!

And what about those with gifts of healing? In some countries, you can't even leave the healing service without a police escort, as thousands of people converge on you. They just want a touch from the man of God. And what about those with other supernatural gifts, like prophecy? People will travel thousands of miles to have an audience with you in hopes that you will have a word for them. That is power!

The danger here is that we can think the power is coming from us, which makes us think *we* are something special. This leads to catering to our flesh rather than crucifying our flesh. Not only so, but the power we carry can make us very attractive to others, and the next thing you know, we have a following of devoted spiritual groupies. This is a recipe for disaster.

Power can be intoxicating, and when we are intoxicated, we are not vigilant. The enemy comes right in, and we're not even aware. There is also more spiritual attack that comes against you when you move in certain anointings, and if you become complacent in the midst of the attack—or worse still, become arrogant—you will easily be brought down.

Revelatory deception

Sexual temptation is bad enough, but if you add deception to the mix, it's even harder to resist. One megachurch leader claimed that God told him he married the wrong woman, after which he allegedly pressured her to get a divorce, getting married to another woman seven days after the divorce became final. And who performed his new wedding ceremony? A pastor who himself was later caught in adultery. Is it any wonder that, according to Jesus Himself, it was a false prophetess whom church leaders permitted "to teach and seduce My servants to commit sexual immorality and eat food sacrificed to idols" (Rev. 2:20)? And note again the connection between sexual immorality and idolatry.

It's true that non-Charismatics will be tempted to sin just as Charismatics are tempted to sin, but they are less likely to use "the Lord told me" as an excuse to sin. It's amazing what we can "hear" when the flesh really wants something!

A professor at a Christian university was approached by a couple after he spoke one night, and they asked him to pray over them. As he was about to lay hands on them, the professor felt something wasn't right, so he stopped and asked, "You're married, right?" They shook their heads and said, "Yes, we're married."

Again he went to pray, but something still felt off in his spirit, so he asked them an odd-sounding question, "You're married *to each other*, right?" To his shock they replied, "No, we're each married to someone else, but the divorces have almost gone through, and we know that the Lord is blessing our relationship, since we pray in tongues before we're together and we really feel His presence." Only among us Charismatics do you hear nonsense like that.

May God deliver us from deception by the truth of His holy Word. And may He gift more of His servants with greater discernment, just like this university professor who knew something was wrong.

Interestingly in this bizarre example you see both the weaknesses and strengths of our movement: weaknesses in that some of us are so grossly (and willfully) deceived and strengths in that the Holy Spirit exposes the deception.

Doctrinal sloppiness

A Facebook friend of mine wrote to me, sharing his frustration after a lengthy exchange with a Nigerian minister. This friend is in ministry himself and absolutely believes in the gifts and power of the Spirit. But he despises the doctrinal sloppiness that is so often found in our midst (see chapter 9), and he relentlessly attacks it in his speaking and online commenting.

He summarized the position of this Nigerian leader as follows: "You know it; you cannot lose the anointing. The flesh is dead, you are a new creation, and sex cannot make you lose your anointing. The Bible is very clear on this, and the Bible cannot lie. You see, you are spirit, and you minister by the Spirit, but your body is flesh. So whatever you do with your flesh cannot affect your spiritual power."

My Facebook friend continued, "Nigeria is *right now* massively invaded by ultra-false grace, really witchcraft in the fellowships, touting, 'Sexual relations do not affect your spirit. You cannot lose your anointing.'" What a deadly deception!

The obvious truth is that what you do in your body affects your life and ministry; we are whole people—spirit, soul, and body. And even if, technically speaking, you can't lose your anointing because of your sin,[8] you can lose your reputation, you can lose your integrity, you can lose your ministry, and you can lose your soul.

My friend also wrote this: "Nigeria, I found, has *very righteous brothers and sisters*, and as one brother told me, also followers of Pastor ____ gone bad, out for money, cars, mansions, and girls. They preach, 'Do whatever; you cannot lose your anointing,' which allows everyone to have sex. 'But no,' they say, 'I am not telling anyone to sin, but sex is outside our spirit, and we have grace, so we cannot lose our anointing.'"

In my book *Hyper-Grace* I warned about abuses such as this. The difference is that today the abuses are even more extreme than when *Hyper-Grace* was published in 2014.

Lack of accountability

Being part of a denomination does not guarantee doctrinal soundness or moral purity, and leaders can find ways to evade accountability if they so desire. But because so many of our Charismatic churches are independent, and because so many are led by forceful leaders, we often have a recipe for extreme unaccountability.

I heard one megachurch pastor explain that when he didn't like the way things were being done in his organization, he fired his entire board. They had no recourse against him and no way of holding him accountable for his actions, meaning he could steal money or sleep around, get caught, then fire his board and claim he was the victim. That is how he structured his organization.

I learned of another pastor who grew wealthy through his abusive financial arrangement with his church. When he first started, there were very few people, and he had almost no money to live on, so he needed to receive almost everything that came in just to survive. At that time, the arrangement was made that he would receive 90 percent of the church income, after expenses (like renting a building), which was still not enough to live on. But as time went on and the church prospered, the arrangement remained the same, and he became rich in the process while the congregation struggled. It's mind-boggling that something like this could happen, but it did, all because of an unaccountable, abusive leadership style.

Need I explain how this kind of mind-set and leadership style opens the door wide to sexual sin? Need I explain how lack of accountability is a seedbed for moral failure? To the extent I believe I will not get caught, to that extent I think I can get away with anything. To the extent I feel that no one can hold me accountable for my deeds, to that extent I am digging my own spiritual grave and to that extent I forget that I will one day give account to God.

Here are some important reminders from the Word for us all:

- "Do not fear those who kill the body but are not able to kill the soul. But rather fear Him who is able to destroy both soul and body in hell" (the words of Jesus in Matthew 10:28).
- "For we must all appear before the judgment seat of Christ, that each one may receive his recompense in the body, according to what he has done, whether it was good or bad" (2 Cor. 5:10).

- "For we shall all stand before the judgment seat of Christ. For it is written: 'As I live, says the Lord, every knee shall bow to Me, and every tongue shall confess to God.' So then each of us shall give an account of himself to God" (Rom. 14:10–12).
- "Not many of you should become teachers, my brothers, for you know that we who teach will be judged with greater strictness" (James 3:1, ESV).
- "As for those [elders] who persist in sin, rebuke them in the presence of all, so that the rest may stand in fear" (1 Tim. 5:20, ESV).

And consider this final warning from the Lord Jesus, who has entrusted His "little ones" to our care:

> But if you cause one of these little ones who trusts in me to fall into sin, it would be better for you to have a large millstone tied around your neck and be drowned in the depths of the sea.
>
> What sorrow awaits the world, because it tempts people to sin. Temptations are inevitable, but what sorrow awaits the person who does the tempting.
>
> So if your hand or foot causes you to sin, cut it off and throw it away. It's better to enter eternal life with only one hand or one foot than to be thrown into eternal fire with both of your hands and feet. And if your eye causes you to sin, gouge it out and throw it away. It's better to enter eternal life with only one eye than to have two eyes and be thrown into the fire of hell.
>
> Beware that you don't look down on any of these little ones. For I tell you that in heaven their angels are always in the presence of my heavenly Father.
>
> —MATTHEW 18:6–10, NLT

Much has been given to us, and much is required of us. May we walk worthy of our high calling in God. It is not just our lives that depend on it. The lives of those we minister to depend on it as well.

Chapter Eight
The Pep-Talk, Prosperity Gospel

One of my closest friends is a highly respected Christian leader in India, a man who has planted more than seven thousand churches in unreached tribal regions as well as built schools, orphanages, hospitals, homes for the elderly, and training centers for the disabled. His work has been so effective that it has been recognized by the government, even helping to bring regional transformation. He also has pioneered effective gospel works in other nations. Yet he was raised an untouchable, almost died of malnutrition as a boy, and became a violent, alcoholic, atheistic communist before Jesus appeared to him in a vision when my friend was in his early twenties. He was instantly born again and began preaching Jesus on the streets. His name is Yesupadam, which means "Jesus foot," a name his Christian father gave him and a name he hated before he was saved.[1]

On one occasion he was stoned for preaching the gospel in a hostile Hindu village, but not long after that the elders of that village came to him—these were the very men who stoned him—wanting to follow Jesus themselves. Many years later I had a meal in the home of one of these men. He was now pastoring a local church in that very area. Jesus truly saves and transforms!

When Yesupadam started his ministry, he had no support at all and was quite poor, yet he stepped out in faith, caring for needy children and preaching the gospel to the lost, and God provided for him. Today, when you see the extent of the work the Lord is doing through him in India, it is breathtaking and inspiring.

But he has seen the same spiritual principles at work in countries such as Germany, Canada, and Madagascar. In fact, in Madagascar, a large island off the coast of Africa marked by great poverty, one of Yesupadam's spiritual sons is building schools, feeding the hungry, and planting churches. And after Yesupadam preached in a large jail there, so many inmates came to faith that the authorities asked him to construct a church building right in the heart of the jail. Yes, a church building in a jail! Inmates meet there every day, getting saved and growing in the Lord. It is the nicest building, by far, in the jail.

So Yesupadam knows about the abundant supply of God, as his ministry provides several thousand meals a day, along with housing, clothing, and education for many hundreds of children, women, and men. Plus, he constantly takes on massive new faith projects. Yet when I asked him what was the greatest abuse in the Charismatic church of India, he answered immediately, "The prosperity gospel." This is the same message that has done so much harm in (and, tragically, been exported from) the United States. It is the same message that has spread like a plague in Africa and that is now making a negative impact in India (among other nations and continents).

It is the message that claims that Jesus died to make you financially rich, that states you can measure your spirituality by your earthly possessions, that encourages you to focus on material prosperity, that declares that the gospel is good news to the poor because it promises them riches. What an utter perversion of the gospel of Jesus, and what a serious deviation from the message of the cross.

Do I believe in divine provision? Absolutely. Do I believe God entrusts earthly riches to some of His people? Without a doubt.

Do I believe material blessings are sometimes a reflection of spiritual blessings? Certainly. Do I believe the gospel can lift the poor up from the garbage dump? Definitely. But I do not believe in the carnal prosperity message, one that takes our eyes off the cross, ignores the message of death to the flesh, and makes Jesus into the sure-fire path to financial success.

Listen to how strongly Paul warned against this very mind-set.

> But godliness with contentment is great gain. For we brought nothing into this world, and it is certain that we can carry nothing out. If we have food and clothing, we shall be content with these things. But those who desire to be rich fall into temptation and a snare and into many foolish and harmful lusts, which drown men in ruin and destruction. For the love of money is the root of all evil. While coveting after money, some have strayed from the faith and pierced themselves through with many sorrows. But you, O man of God, escape these things, and follow after righteousness, godliness, faith, love, patience, and gentleness.
>
> —1 Timothy 6:6–11

What a different message is preached today, a carnal message, a worldly message, a message that brings lots of money to the big leaders who preach it and robs God's people along the way. It is a message that leads to bizarre scenes such as the one I saw on YouTube, where hundreds of believers ran to the altar in a frenzy, throwing piles of money in the direction of the pastor standing in front of them while shouting, "Money cometh to me!" And they're doing all this because they believe that as they give, their debts will be supernaturally cancelled. They would do far better taking a course on godly financial stewardship.

In my 1990 book *How Saved Are We?* I devoted a whole chapter to the subject of the carnal prosperity gospel. Allow me to repeat some of it here:

> This is what has happened to our modern day prosperity gospel: *it has run aground on the shallow shores of greed and ambition; it has capsized in the turbulent waters of selfishness; it has sunk under the weight of covetous hearts.* May it never sail again!
>
> How could we be so blind? We have encouraged people to "want to get rich." We have told them that it is all right to be "eager for money." We have taught carnally minded believers who have not died to the world to pursue worldly wealth. And we try to make the whole thing so spiritual, as if the reason God exists is to meet all our wants. Some even teach: "You can have whatever you say, so just speak it out all the time -- a swimming pool, a giant screen TV, a mink stole. The Lord wants you to have an abundant life!" And now many of us are trapped. We have taken our eyes off Jesus and put them on earthly treasures. The "deceitfulness of wealth" has tricked us again. It has stolen eternity from our hearts! Some of us have even become "fools" -- we have stored up things for ourselves but are not rich toward God (Luke 12:20-21).
>
> Two thousand years ago Jesus sounded an alarm: "Watch out! *Be on your guard against all kinds of greed*; a man's life does not consist in the abundance of his possessions" (Luke 12:15). Yet today we glorify greed and sanctify selfishness -- under the guise of great faith. We measure heavenly blessing by earthly bounty and equate real spirituality with financial success. Have we forgotten that "God has chosen those who are poor in the eyes of the world to be rich in faith and to inherit the kingdom He promised those who love Him" (Jam. 2:5)? Do we realize that "what is highly valued among men is

> detestable in God's sight" (Luke 16:15)? It is the man who lives for riches who "will fade away even while he goes about his business" (Jam. 1:11). Let us cleanse our hearts now of all covetousness!
>
> James accused his readers of being adulterous people, friends with the world. This was one of their symptoms. "When you ask, you do not receive, because you ask with wrong motives, *that you may spend what you get on your pleasures*" (Jam. 4:3). Yet our new teaching has fostered such praying! We have given it biblical support. Today we really know how to "use the Word" -- to get new cars and diamond rings! *And we actually think all this is spiritual.* God have mercy on us!
>
> There is so much idolatry in our midst. How much longer can we survive? Paul said that a greedy person is an idolater, and that idolaters do not enter the kingdom of God (Eph. 5:5). Are we selling our inheritance for a piece of bread?
>
> No -- there is nothing wrong with having possessions. But there is something wrong with possessions having us! There is nothing wrong with being rich -- as long as being rich is not the purpose of our being! We cannot serve both God and Money (Mat. 6:24).[2]

But something has changed in the years since I wrote *How Saved Are We?* The prosperity gospel has been joined to the pep-talk gospel, taking us even further from the cross.

What exactly is the pep-talk gospel? It is a feel-good, motivational message, and nothing more. It lifts you up and cheers you up and puts a smile on your face without ever calling you to turn from sin, without ever confronting you with the consequences of disobedience, without ever talking about judgment or God's wrath. That is not the gospel.

According to this gospel, sadness is your adversary, not sin.

Depression is your enemy, not depravity. Jesus doesn't want you to feel bad, but He's not calling you to turn from sin. That is the pep-talk gospel. Happiness, not holiness, is the goal.

Years ago I expressed my thoughts on this so-called gospel message in a short poem called "Pablum From the Pit." For the first time, here it is printed in a book:

Pablum From the Pit

Cootchie, cootchie, cootchie coo,
God loves me and God loves you!
Smile sinner, don't be sad;
God's not angry; He's not mad.
Even when you leave the path,
There's no hell and there's no wrath.
So don't you fear, just do your best.
Judgment Day won't be a test.
God sees your heart and that's enough.
The Judgment Seat won't be that tough.
For you can't sin away His grace
Or take that smile from His face.
'Cause God is love and love is good:
He'll treat you like you think He should!
Just trust me, sinner, to the end.
My name is Satan; I'm your friend.

Does this sound familiar? Have you heard this woefully imbalanced message yourself?

Like many of you, I've been a student of the Word for decades, and I've gone through the New Testament over and over again. So here's a simple challenge to my fellow lovers of the Word: Please show me this pep-talk message anywhere in the Scriptures. Please show it to me in the words of Jesus or Paul or John or Peter or Jacob (James) or Judah (Jude). Please show it to me in the words of Moses or the prophets or the Psalms or Proverbs. Please show it to me in the Word of God.

Do I find promises of abundant provision in the Bible? I sure do. Do I find encouragement in the Scriptures? Day and night. Do I find comfort and hope and inspiration? Seven days a week, twenty-four hours a day. Do I find life and blessing and joy? Yes, yes, and yes! But I also find stern warnings and strong exhortations and sobering examples, and I find serious calls for repentance and reformation, with severe consequences for noncompliance. This is found from Genesis to Revelation, and there is no way under the sun that anyone could preach a pep-talk gospel while preaching through the entire Bible. Not a chance. There's no way anyone could do it while preaching through just the New Testament or the Gospels or the letters of Paul, let alone preaching through the Book of Revelation. Simply stated, *there is no such thing as a biblically based pep-talk gospel.*

It is very possible that some pep-talk preachers are motivated by love and want to help those who are downtrodden and discouraged. But true love tells the truth, and at some point we have to tell people the rest of the story, namely that God is a holy and jealous God, that He requires all that we have, and that one day we will give an account to Him. We must tell them that Jesus is our Lord and Master and that He calls us to take up our own cross and follow Him. We must teach them about mercy *and* judgment, about the kindness *and* severity of God, about heaven *and* hell. We must help them to understand what sin is in God's sight and how, through the blood of Jesus, we have the full and complete antidote to sin. This is more than just a motivational pep talk! As Paul urged the Gentile believers in Rome, "Consider the goodness and severity of God—severity toward those who fell, but goodness toward you, if you continue in His goodness. Otherwise, you also will be cut off" (Rom. 11:22).

The "Success in Life" Gospel

If you listen to some preachers today, the goal of the gospel can be summed up in one word: *success*. And you can measure your spirituality by your outward success in life. How much money do you make every week? How far have you climbed on the social ladder? How big is your wardrobe? How expensive is your car? How much fame do you have? That is how spiritual you are!

I wonder how Paul would have measured up to this. As he wrote to the Corinthians:

> We give no offense in anything, that our service may not be blamed. But in all things we commend ourselves as servants of God: in much patience, in afflictions, in necessities, in distress, in stripes, in imprisonments, in tumults, in labors, in sleeplessness, and in hunger; by purity, by knowledge, by patience, by kindness, by the Holy Spirit, by genuine love, by the word of truth, by the power of God, by the armor of righteousness on the right hand and on the left, by honor and dishonor, by evil report and good report; as deceivers, and yet true; as unknown, and yet well known; as dying, and look, we live; as punished, but not killed; as sorrowful, yet always rejoicing; as poor, yet making many rich; and as having nothing, and yet possessing all things.
>
> —2 CORINTHIANS 6:3–10

Was Paul missing something? Did he not have enough faith? Or is it possible he was far more successful than the vast majority of people who ever walked this planet, including kings and presidents and celebrities and generals—and I mean truly successful?

In the early 1980s I heard a story about a Chinese Christian leader who had been tortured for his faith then was released from prison and made his way to America. He was attending a conference featuring some well-known preachers when a pastor came up to him and rebuked him for his lack of faith—because he was wearing a shabby suit. Can you imagine this? This American pastor was so carnally minded that he thought this spiritual giant from China, a man who endured torture for the gospel without denying Jesus, was lacking in faith because he wasn't wearing a flashy outfit.

Back in the 1990s I was so grieved by this kind of mentality that I wrote a sarcastic poem titled "Whither Persecution?" Here it is, also printed in a book for the first time:

Whither Persecution?

Persecuted saints? Oh no, not in our day.
We are the enlightened church; we've found a better way
To preach the gospel message while getting no one mad:
We leave out "God the Judge" and just speak of "God the Dad"!
We major on the promises. We're positive to the max.
We want the sinner to feel at home. We help him to relax!
We're strong on self-acceptance; we build the ego up;
We're here to make you happy—so come to church and sup!
You'll find such tasty dainties; each meal will be so sweet;
Nothing will upset you; the sermon will be a treat!
Sunday morning is the best show, designed to entertain,
With every detail chosen to spare the rebel pain.
We've cut out all those nasty words: "hell," "repent," and "sin";
Our pastor's slick, with such finesse; even his wardrobe's in!
He's not the John the Baptist type, rabid and out of control,

Raving and foaming at the mouth, like some
frenzied droll.
Our church is for the family, with fashion shows
and fun;
And bowling, tennis, swimming, too, plus cruises in
the sun.
We're socially acceptable; we adapt and change our hue;
We're sensitive to our culture—like chameleons we're
true blue!
Oh, away from us, you dreary ones with your talk of
self-denial;
Jesus already bore the cross; now we can live in style!
The Savior's not offensive; He only gives good things.
He makes us rich and prosperous so we can reign
as kings!
Suffering, hardship, martyrdom—they're really not for us.
We're giving out the good news. There's no need for all
the fuss!
Persecution comes from lack of faith, when saints don't
know the Word;
Poor Stephen might be alive today, if our message he'd
only heard....

Since I wrote that poem, millions of Christians have been killed, beaten, tortured, imprisoned, or exiled for their faith while we're still measuring our spirituality by the type of vehicle we drive or the amount of money in our bank accounts or the size of the house we live in. What universe are we living in?

And what do we do with verses such as these, from the lips of Jesus, Paul, and Peter?

- "Blessed are you when men revile you, and persecute you, and say all kinds of evil against you falsely for My sake. Rejoice and be very glad, because great is your reward in heaven, for in this manner they persecuted the prophets who were before you" (Matt. 5:11–12).

- "I have told you these things so that in Me you may have peace. In the world you will have tribulation. But be of good cheer. I have overcome the world" (John 16:33).
- "When they had preached the gospel to that city and had made many disciples, they returned to Lystra and to Iconium and to Antioch, strengthening the minds of the disciples and exhorting them to continue in the faith, to go through many afflictions and thus enter the kingdom of God" (Acts 14:21–22).
- "The Spirit Himself bears witness with our spirits that we are the children of God, and if children, then heirs: heirs of God and joint-heirs with Christ, if indeed we suffer with Him, that we may also be glorified with Him. For I consider that the sufferings of this present time are not worthy to be compared with the glory which shall be revealed to us" (Rom. 8:16–18).
- "Who shall separate us from the love of Christ? Shall tribulation, or distress, or persecution, or famine, or nakedness, or peril, or sword? As it is written: 'For Your sake we are killed all day long; we are counted as sheep for the slaughter.' No, in all these things we are more than conquerors through Him who loved us" (Rom. 8:35–37).

- "Beloved, do not be surprised at the fiery ordeal that is taking place among you to test you, as though some strange thing happened to you. But rejoice insofar as you share in Christ's sufferings, so that you may rejoice and be glad also in the revelation of His glory.... [And] after you have suffered a little while, the God of all grace, who has called us to His eternal glory through Christ Jesus, will restore, support, strengthen, and establish you" (1 Pet. 4:12–13; 5:10–11).

Somehow these verses—all of which speak of suffering persecution, opposition, and hardship for the gospel—do not mesh well with the success-in-life, pep-talk, hyper-prosperity message.

To repeat: I believe in God's provision, and over the years millions of dollars have gone through our ministry to support the work of the gospel around the world. And I thank God for meeting my family's needs and giving us a beautiful home to live in. But it doesn't take great faith to live in a nice house. It takes great faith to believe for your crops to grow in the midst of a drought as your neighbors die around you. And it doesn't take great faith to get people to give you money when you promise them riches in return. But it does take great faith to confess Jesus as Lord when you are promised imprisonment and death in return.

"If God Loves Me, Why Am I Poor?"

At the time of this writing I host several different TV shows on three different networks (GOD TV, Middle East TV, and NRB TV), along with my daily radio broadcast. One of my shows on GOD TV is called *Ask Me Anything*, where I respond to questions sent in from viewers around the world. More than once someone from India has asked, "If God loves me, why am I poor?" This is some of the effect of the carnal prosperity message, since most people hearing it around the world are poor, and after hearing the message and sending in their sacrificial gift, they remain poor. They have not become rich like the fancy preacher on TV.

But rather than question whether God loves them, these precious believers should take comfort in the words of Jacob (James), who wrote: "Listen, my beloved brothers. Has God not chosen the poor of this world to be rich in faith and heirs of the kingdom which He has promised to those who love Him? But you have despised the poor. Do not rich men oppress you and drag you before the judgment seats? Do they not blaspheme that worthy name by which you are called?" (James 2:5–7).

Throughout Scripture there are far more rebukes for the rich than for the poor, along with far more warnings. Conversely, Jesus identifies with the poor and needy. (See Matthew 25:31–46.) And I write this as someone who, by global standards, would be considered rich as a middle class (or upper-middle class) American. One godly woman who works with the very poor in Africa heard the Lord say to her, "Come up here where I am, with the poor." Yes, come *up* here, where the poor are. How different this is from our earthly perspective.

After Jesus said to the religious leaders, "You cannot serve God and wealth," Luke tells us. "The Pharisees, who were lovers of money, heard all these things and derided Him. He said to them, 'You are those who justify yourselves before men, but God knows your hearts. *For that which is highly esteemed before men is an abomination before God*'" (Luke 16:13–15, emphasis added). That's why the Lord taught a parable to warn the person "who stores up treasure for himself, and is not rich toward God" (Luke 12:21). And that's why John exhorted: "Do not love the world or the things in the world. If anyone loves the world, the love of the Father is not in him. For all that is in the world—the lust of the flesh, the lust of the eyes, and the pride of life—is not of the Father, but is of the world. The world and its desires are passing away, but the one who does the will of God lives forever" (1 John 2:15–17).

It's interesting that, in the Book of Revelation, Jesus rebuked congregations that were rich in this world and poor toward God while commending those who had little in this world but were rich in God. To the Laodiceans He said, "For you say, 'I am rich, and have stored up goods, and have need of nothing,' yet do not realize that you are wretched, miserable, poor, blind, and naked. I counsel you to buy from Me gold refined by fire, that you may be rich, and white garments, that you may be dressed, that the shame of your nakedness may not appear, and anoint your eyes with eye salve, that you may see" (Rev. 3:17–18). In contrast, He said to the believers in Smyrna, "I know your works and tribulation and poverty (but you are rich)" (Rev. 2:9).

I know all the verses cited to support a carnal prosperity gospel, and I affirm the truth of what those verses do teach, namely that God meets our needs (Ps. 37:25; Phil. 4:19); that as we give with generosity, we receive a generous return (Prov. 3:9–10; Luke 6:38; 2 Cor. 9:6–11); that financial prosperity is sometimes a sign of divine favor (Deut. 28:1–4; Prov. 22:4); and that poverty, in and of itself, is a curse not a blessing (Deut. 28:15–19). But I do not believe that Jesus died on the cross to make us financially rich, I do not believe that spiritual blessing is always manifest in outward success, and I do not believe that we should encourage God's people to set their hearts on earthly riches. Jesus flatly warned against this. (See Matthew 6:19–24.)

What's interesting is that I have preached in some of the wealthiest, most giving churches in the world, and they do not preach a carnal prosperity gospel. And I know some very successful businessmen who ask God for His blessing on their work every single day, and they do not preach a carnal prosperity gospel. And I know some of the most dynamic, faith-based ministries on the globe, and they do not preach a carnal prosperity gospel. I truly hope and pray that you can see and hear the difference between living by faith in God's provision for God's purposes, and believing a carnal prosperity message.

One of the largest churches in Nigeria has built a whole complex of schools and apartments, and established programs to help the poor and needy. It is making a real social impact, and it is doing this without the help of foreigners. The pastor of this church told some of my friends his philosophy regarding finances, using this story as an illustration.

A young man came to the pastor for prayer. He was a college graduate with a degree in engineering, but he couldn't find any work. He asked the pastor to pray that he would get a job, but the pastor refused, since the young man was not currently working. This confused him, as he said he wasn't working because he couldn't find a job. The pastor said, "Well, you can do something. You can always find work."

The pastor then asked him if he had ever seen people on the street selling peanuts. Why not do that? So this young man, with a degree in engineering, began to sell peanuts on the street. Today he owns some of the biggest peanut processing plants in his country and is a multi-millionaire, regularly attending the same church and giving generously. The pastor said he has many such stories he could share, based on people working hard, using their gifts in the business world, and then giving with generosity.

The same friends who shared this story with me also gave me some good news about what is happening in Nigeria. They told me that when the prosperity message came to their country, it came in the worst form, with all its extremes, doing lots of damage. But now, they said, it has moderated, focusing more on biblical truths about sowing and reaping. So a course correction is being made, at least in part. This is good news indeed, but it will take some time to undo the damage and further expose the error, which is still being propagated there.

Ironically, when some of my African friends have come to the States, they have been shocked at the believers' lack of spirituality—at our prayerlessness and carnality and worldliness and lack of faith in God's power. A brother from Ghana once commented to a colleague of mine, "No wonder you see so little happening in your country. You spend all your time feasting; we spend ours fasting."

So the wake-up call cuts both ways. And to be candid, when it comes to the concerns of our African brothers for the church of America, those concerns would be even greater for non-Charismatic churches, since, as I mentioned before, even Baptist churches in Africa commonly pray for the sick and drive out demons. It looks like all of us could use some healthy self-examination here, and perhaps we need to look at the bigger issue at play: an ear-tickling, watered-down, compromised "gospel."

Five Signs of an Ear-Tickling, Carnal Gospel

Paul warned Timothy that "the time will come when people will not endure sound doctrine, but they will gather to themselves teachers in accordance with their own desires, having itching ears, and they will turn their ears away from the truth and turn to myths" (2 Tim. 4:3–4). That warning proved true in Timothy's day, and it has proved true many times since, especially today, when we have a multitude of ear-tickling preachers. How can we recognize them?

We know that deception is very deceiving and that no one is willingly duped. And we know that no one stands up and says, "What I'm teaching is false doctrine meant to deceive and destroy you!" We also know that it is arrogant for any of us to think that we alone have sound doctrine while everyone else is in error. Yet Paul did not warn Timothy in vain, nor is he warning us in vain. So we must ask ourselves what exactly are the distinguishing characteristics of ear-tickling preachers.[3]

1. Ear-tickling preachers bypass self-denial and the cross.

Jesus told His disciples that if anyone wanted to follow Him, they had to deny themselves and take up the cross. (See Matthew 16:24; Mark 8:34; and Luke 9:23, in which Jesus says we must take up our cross daily.) And Paul taught that "those who belong to Christ Jesus have crucified the flesh with its passions and desires" (Gal. 5:24, ESV).

Saying no to self and taking up the cross—meaning, giving up the claim to our own lives, dying to this sinful world, and renouncing its claims—is a fundamental part of discipleship. Yet ear-tickling preachers will not talk about it. The reason is obvious: it is not what our flesh wants to hear.

2. Ear-tickling preachers go light on sin.

Throughout the Scriptures, in both the Old and New Testaments, the Gospels, Acts, the letters, and Revelation, there are warnings about the dangers of sin and calls to turn away from sin. Of course it is absolutely true that through the death and resurrection of Jesus and by the power of the Spirit we have been given victory over sin. And it is absolutely true that the message of grace, rightly understood, turns us away from sin. (See Titus 2:11–14.)

But that doesn't mean leaders no longer need to warn their hearers about the deceitfulness of sin or urge them to be vigilant against sin. To the contrary, because so much grace has been given to us, a leader's responsibility before God is even greater. (See Hebrews 2:1–4; 10:26–31; and 12:25–29).

3. Ear-tickling preachers are loved by the world.

In 2 Timothy 3 Paul recounted the persecutions and suffering he endured for the gospel—they were frequent and intense—and then said, "Indeed, all who desire to live a godly life in Christ Jesus will be persecuted, while evil people and impostors will go on from bad to worse, deceiving and being deceived" (2 Tim. 3:12–13, ESV).

Jesus said the world would treat us the way it treated Him (John 15:18; Matt. 10:24–25) and that His disciples, like the prophets of old, would be persecuted for righteousness' sake (Matt. 5:10–12). "If you were of the world," He said, "the world would love you as its own; but because you are not of the world, but I chose you out of the world, therefore the world hates you" (John 15:19, ESV). But the world doesn't hate ear-tickling preachers because they are "of the world" in their approach to the gospel.

It is one thing to have a good reputation of integrity and purity and to live out what we preach. It is another thing when our message does not offend sinners. As Jesus warned, "Woe to you, when all people speak well of you, for so their fathers did to the false prophets" (Luke 6:26, ESV).

4. Ear-tickling preachers tell the flesh what it wants to hear.

The Old Testament prophets had to deal with this all the time. As Isaiah wrote long ago, "For they are a rebellious people, lying children, children unwilling to hear the instruction of the LORD; who say to the seers, 'Do not see,' and to the prophets, 'Do not prophesy to us what is right; speak to us smooth things, prophesy illusions, leave the way, turn aside from the path, let us hear no more about the Holy One of Israel.'" (Isa. 30:9–11, ESV). In other words, "Don't make us uncomfortable, preacher! Don't make us squirm! Stop confronting us with the standards of a holy God!"

A friend recently shared with me that he learned the owner

of a local strip club was attending the same church that he and his family attended. His sister-in-law approached the pastor and asked him about it, and the pastor said, "At least he's coming to church. That's better than not coming at all."

That would be true, except that the pastor never said a word about sin and never said anything that would make the man uncomfortable about his exploitation of young women (and others). And so rather than this man getting convicted of his sins and discovering the life-changing love of God, he went home deceived. Ultimately, my friend and his family had to leave.

For good reason the late author and evangelist Leonard Ravenhill said, "If Jesus preached the same message ministers preach today, He would have never been crucified."[4]

5. Ear-tickling preachers do not live in the light of eternity.

The message they preach works fine without any future hope since this world is our place of blessing and prosperity. Who needs the encouragement of the world to come? Who needs the comfort of future glory? We already have everything we need here and now!

Paul saw it very differently, writing to the Corinthians, "If in this life only we have hope in Christ, we are of all men most miserable" (1 Cor. 15:19). He also wrote to the Romans that we "who have the first fruits of the Spirit, groan within ourselves while eagerly waiting for adoption, the redemption of our bodies. For we are saved through hope, but hope that is seen is not hope, for why does a man still hope for what he sees? But if we hope for what we do not see, we wait for it with patience" (Rom. 8:23–25). And once more Paul said to the Corinthians:

> For this reason we do not lose heart: Even though our outward man is perishing, yet our inward man is being renewed day by day. Our light affliction, which lasts but

> for a moment, works for us a far more exceeding and eternal weight of glory, while we do not look at the things which are seen, but at the things which are not seen. For the things which are seen are temporal, but the things which are not seen are eternal.
>
> —2 CORINTHIANS 4:16–18

For the pep-talk, carnal prosperity preachers this world is more than enough. Eternity is out of sight, out of mind. Who needs a heavenly hope with all the earthly riches we already have?

I personally believe there are preachers today who genuinely know the Lord but have bought into a lie about the nature of the gospel. And while they think they are helping people, they are really hurting them in the long run. May God grant these men and women repentance, may He expose the real charlatans and deceivers, and may He give us discernment, humility, and a love for the truth, regardless of cost or consequence.

Enough with this pep-talk, carnal gospel. The real gospel—the gospel of Jesus—is more than enough, for this world and the world to come.

Chapter Nine
Celebrating Doctrinal Deviance

Do you remember how the Athenians are described in Acts 17:21? "For all the Athenians and foreigners who lived there spent their time in nothing else, but either telling or hearing something new." That sounds like some of us! Our ears are itching to hear something new, something exotic, something different, something really out there and edgy. That's what we love to hear. Don't bore us with that old-fashioned message of holiness, discipleship, prayer, outreach, and worship. *Give us something new.*

Years ago I gently confronted a traveling prophet and teacher with the permission of the Bible school where he was ministering (and where I also taught). The students were asking me about some of his messages, which sounded totally off base, so Nancy went to hear him teach one day and took copious notes. Although she didn't know Hebrew or Greek, she knew what he was saying was wrong. To this day, now more than three decades later, we still remember one of the questions she asked me incredulously when she got home from hearing him teach: "Is the Hebrew word for womb *embryo-mamaya*?" Honestly! Who could even make this up?

I recall that he also claimed that in Luke 13:32, where Jesus referred to Herod as a "fox," He actually meant Herod was gay. I've checked dozens of commentaries and lexicons and have never found any confirmation for his claim about the word *fox*. Where did he get this from?

I made an appointment to meet with this brother and politely challenged some of his statements based on my intimate knowledge of the Hebrew and my familiarity with the Greek. After he questioned whether or not I knew what I was talking about, he moved on to the crux of the issue. He told me that for years he was a basic, ABC gospel teacher, and no one came to his meetings. Now, he said, with all the Hebrew and Greek nuggets he gave them, they came flocking to hear him. "The people love it," he said to me.

His messages were also characterized by what I sarcastically called "the tangent anointing," which works something like this: "Trees are important, because every tree has bark, and you know a dog by its bark, and dogs are a man's best friend, and where would we be without friends, so trees are important." That's about how scattered his sermons were—the one time I heard him preach an entire message, I found it utterly incoherent—yet the people took notes voraciously, devouring his every word, only to repeat his errors to others. To paraphrase the words of Acts, "All too often we Charismatics spend our time in nothing else but either telling or hearing something new."

I know of one preacher who based his ministry on a single Greek word, which he misunderstood and misused. But he became famous for his amazing insights. What kind of dangerous game is this? Is the Bible like a piece of clay that we can shape and mold to our liking? Are the biblical languages like Lego blocks that we can build into anything we desire?

Nancy and I were at a meeting one time when a highly respected teacher shared with the audience what a native Greek speaker allegedly told him about the word "groanings" in Romans 8:26. The verse says, "Likewise, the Spirit helps us in our weaknesses, for we do not know what to pray for as we ought, but the Spirit Himself intercedes for us with groanings too deep for words." According to this teacher, his Greek-speaking source told him the word translated "groanings" was highly unusual and described an utterance that would be similar to tongues, which was the point this speaker was making: Paul was writing here about speaking in tongues.

Now, it's certainly possible that Paul included tongues here in the Spirit's intercession, and I've experienced this many times myself, groaning and travailing in tongues. But the Greek word translated "groanings" is not mysterious at all. It's the word *stenagmos*, which occurs in Acts 7:34, speaking of the groaning of the Israelites in Egypt, as well as twenty-eight more times in the Septuagint, the Greek translation of the Old Testament and Apocrypha, for a total of thirty occurrences. There's nothing unusual or mysterious about the word at all. Not only so, but a few verses earlier, in Romans 8:22 Paul used a related verb meaning "to groan together," while in Romans 8:23, he used the verb "to groan" (*stenazō*, which is directly related to the noun *stenagmos*).

So in Romans 8:22 Paul speaks of all creation *groaning together*; then in 8:23, he speaks of our *groaning* as believers; then in 8:26, he speaks of the Spirit's intercession through us with "*groanings* too deep for words." Even if you didn't know a word of Greek, the context is totally clear, and there's nothing mysterious about it.[1] Of course, the subject itself is incredibly deep—the Spirit makes intercession to the Father through us!—but the Greek is quite straightforward. Unfortunately in some of our Charismatic circles, straightforward teaching doesn't sell. We need some hot new revelation.

In that same conference Nancy and were I listening to another message by this speaker, which overall was quite good, as it had a clear flow of thought. (In other words, he didn't have the "tangent anointing.") At one point in his sermon, he said to the audience, "If anyone tells you God is not good, you point them to Nahum 1:7: "The LORD is good, a strong hold in the day of trouble; and he knoweth them that trust in him" (KJV). His point was that God is not some angry and vengeful Lord, and this was his proof text.

I turned to Nancy with my Bible open and whispered to her, "Read verses 6 and 8," meaning the verses immediately before and after Nahum 1:7, which he had just quoted. The verses read: "Who can stand before His anger? Who will rise up before His burning wrath? His heat is poured out like fire, and the rocks are broken up before Him.... As a flood running forth, He will bring to an end the distress, and He will pursue His adversaries into darkness." So much for the speaker's point!

If he had said that God pours out judgment on His stubborn, unrepentant adversaries, not on His beloved children, I would have said amen. But his statement was off because he failed to read the verse in context. And I remind you: he was a respected teacher.

He also explained in one session that the original name for the Lord was "Jah," which he got from words like Hallelujah, which is Hebrew for "Praise Yah," Yah being a shortened form of Yahweh. But he thought the name was "Jah" (with the *j* pronounced like the *j* in jar) because it was spelled with a *j* in English, and he failed to realize that the English *j* represents the Hebrew *y*. That, however, was just the beginning. He then explained that the Hebrew word for "seek" was *backwash* (seriously!), which totally mystified me. Where in the world did he get this idea?

I finally realized that he must have used the dictionary in the back of Strong's Concordance, which listed the Hebrew root for "seek" as *baqash*, and when he saw the *q*, he must have assumed it was followed by a *u*, since that's what we normally see in English. And of course, he had no way of knowing that this was just a root form, not the actual verbal form used, which was *biqqesh* (pronounced *bee-keysh*). Anyway, that's the best I could do in figuring out how he made such a ridiculous error, and I looked at Nancy in shock and amusement.

Immediately after the service Nancy asked me what I was going to do, and I said to her, "I'm going back to the hotel room to backwash Jah." That became a private joke between us for some time. Whenever I would go to pray, I'd tell her, "I'm going to backwash Jah." And did I mention that this brother was a respected teacher?

On the positive side, his overall message was good. On the negative side, he butchered the Hebrew, and with no gain at that. (In other words, he didn't even make a new and exciting point. He just butchered the language.) Why?

I'm sure he had lots of wisdom from his years in ministry service. And I'm sure he had many fine insights from the Word. And I believe he was a caring, godly man. But why teach that which you think you know rather than that which you really know? And why build doctrines on isolated verses that have to be ripped out of context? Why base whole messages on supposedly secretive meanings of words that simply don't exist? Is it to give the impression that you're a scholar, or to tickle people's itching ears? Or is it simply a matter of making honest mistakes? Whatever it is, it's epidemic in our midst. "Systematic teaching is boring! Tell us something new, the wilder the better."

Now, it's true that Charismatics do not have a monopoly on doctrinal error. Far from it. There is error and deception throughout the body, and, the truth be told, the non-Charismatics who mock us are guilty of serious doctrinal error themselves. They deny the gifts and power of the Spirit are for today, despite the clear testimony of Scripture.[2] And often their derisive, scornful words sound more like vicious gossip columns than constructive critiques.

But again, we Charismatics can be especially prone to doctrinal error for at least three reasons: First, we often contrast *the mind* with *the Spirit*, as if the two were always at war and as if we have to turn off our minds in order to believe God. Second, it's part of our Pentecostal history to despise seminary training and intellectual approaches to the Bible, because of which many of our leaders are lacking in solid biblical education.[3] Third, we believe the Spirit is still speaking today, which opens us up to the possibility of basing doctrine on extra-biblical revelation.

When we look back to 1 Corinthians, we see that Paul had to address serious doctrinal error during his day as well, specifically the denial of a future bodily resurrection. (See 1 Corinthians 15.) So these challenges have been with us since the earliest days of the church. But, to say it yet again, we Charismatics are often especially prone to these kinds of errors.

In the late 1970s one of my friends was having a hard time understanding how to be baptized in the Spirit and speak in tongues, so he asked a Pentecostal brother for advice. The man said to him, "You just need to disengage your mind."

What dangerous counsel! We don't disengage our minds; we renew our minds (Rom. 12:2). There's quite a difference between the two.

Is it possible for our minds to get in the way of faith? Absolutely. We try to rationalize things and intellectualize things and figure things out, and that's often the opposite of a faith-filled response. Can you imagine what would have happened to many of the miracles of the Bible if the vessels used—from Moses to Elijah to Peter to Paul—stopped to rationalize the divine commands? Divide the sea with your rod, Moses! Tell the priests to put their feet into the Jordan, Joshua! Call down fire from heaven, Elijah! Throw a stick in the water and make the axe head float, Elisha! Get out of the boat and walk on the water, Peter! Tell the lame man to stand to his feet, Paul![4]

In the case of Peter we can see exactly what happened to him. He *did* walk on the water in the midst of a terrible storm and in the middle of the night, "But when he saw the strong wind, he was afraid, and beginning to sink, he cried out, 'Lord, save me!'"

(Matt. 14:30). In other words, when he took his eyes off Jesus and focused on the wind and the waves, he began to sink. Put another way, he took his eyes off the supernatural and put them on the natural; he stopped looking at the invisible and focused on the visible. (See 2 Corinthians 4:16–18 and Hebrews 11:24–25.) This is a faith-killing attitude.

Most Charismatics understand this, recognizing the danger of reading the Word through human eyes and not through the eyes of faith. But again, this doesn't mean that we disengage our minds; it means that we renew our minds according to the truth of God and His Word. If we don't do that, how then can we *love Him* with all our hearts and souls *and minds* (Matt. 22:37)?

When it comes to speaking in tongues for the first time, I understand what this brother was trying to say to my friend. Speaking in tongues is different from speaking in your native language, where you consciously form the words and sentences and sounds. Instead, the Spirit speaks through you, so you yield your voice and your tongue to Him. If you think about it too much or overanalyze it, you might never speak in tongues. But we are not called to become passive and turn off our brains. That's an invitation for all kinds of deception. Instead, we are to *yield* our minds to the Lord, and as we sense the Spirit's prompting, we cooperate with Him in faith. The next thing we know, we're speaking a language we never learned before.

Paul wanted to make sure the Corinthians had solid understanding when it came to the gifts, writing, "Now concerning spiritual gifts, brothers, I do not want you to be ignorant. You know that you were Gentiles, carried away to these dumb idols, however you were led" (1 Cor. 12:1–2). And when it came to speaking in tongues, he wrote:

> For if I pray in an unknown tongue, my spirit prays, but my understanding is unfruitful. What is it then? I will pray with the spirit, and I will pray with the understanding. I will sing with the spirit, and I will sing with the understanding. Otherwise, when you bless with the spirit, how will he who occupies the place of the unlearned say "Amen" at your giving of thanks, seeing he does not understand what you say? For you indeed give thanks well, but the other is not edified.
>
> —1 CORINTHIANS 14:14–17

So we pray with the spirit (or Spirit) *and* we pray with understanding. We also ask God for interpretation to better understand our prayers in the S/spirit. (See 1 Corinthians 14:13.) And we get out of the boat and walk on the water when God tells us to, since we are convinced to the core of our being that whatever He says is good. The key is to renew our minds by the Word and Spirit. As Jesus explained, "God is Spirit, and those who worship Him must worship Him in spirit [or Spirit] and truth" (John 4:24).[5] The two go hand in hand.

But the idea that it's necessary to "disengage our minds" in order to receive the Spirit is nowhere in the Word, and it's an idea that can be deadly. After all, if we have to shut off our minds to receive from God in this case, maybe we have to do it in other cases too. And maybe we have to shut off our minds when the minister tells us to empty our bank account and give the money to him. Those brains of ours can be dangerous. Better not to think at all, just mindlessly comply. *That is not the gospel.*

Open Your Mouth and God Will Fill It?

There was an unspoken tradition in the church where I was saved that if you were truly anointed to preach, you could do so without notes. Didn't Jesus tell His disciples not to give any forethought to how they would respond to kings and rulers when they were brought before them? He said, "You will be brought before governors and kings for My sake, for a testimony against them and the Gentiles. But when they deliver you up, take no thought of how or what you will speak. For it will be given you at that time what you will speak. For it is not you who speak, but the Spirit of your Father who speaks through you" (Matt. 10:18–20). And didn't God say to us in Psalm 81:10, "Open your mouth wide, and I will fill it"? (This verse is taken totally out of context; read it for yourself, and you'll see.)

Well, this put extra pressure on my friends and me when we were first asked to preach in August 1973 at the ages of eighteen, nineteen, and eighteen, respectively. (I was the last to speak.) We were barely (or not even) two years old in the Lord, we had never preached in our lives, no one gave us guidelines about how to put a message together (we could only go by how our pastor preached), and we were not supposed to use notes. If we really wanted to be true to form, we wouldn't even think in advance of what we were going to say!

When it came time for the first message—this was from the bass player of our old rock band—he got up and spoke for about twenty minutes. Afterward he and I named his message "Random Thoughts on Christianity." Exactly! One week later, it was time for the guitar player, and he did great for about five minutes, until he suddenly realized he was preaching from the pulpit in front of forty to fifty people. He got red in the face, stopped speaking, and sat down. One week later, it was my turn, and I actually felt God had dropped a message in my heart a few days earlier. I also had the benefit of having memorized about four thousand verses in the previous six to eight months, so the Word just came pouring out of me, point for point, following Paul's words in Acts 26:18.

To this day I normally preach without notes, but that is based on decades of constant study of the Word, teaching of the Word, and writing about the Word, and it is all empowered by the gracious anointing of the Spirit. But that's also the way the Lord wired and gifted me, and my mind works in a very systematic fashion. For example, if I'm driving in the car and Nancy calls me with a list of a dozen grocery items to get when I stop at the store, I put them in alphabetical order in my head, which helps me to memorize the list. And when I'm praying about the contents of an outline for a class I'm going to teach, once the subject is formed clearly in my head, I can write down the main points for the entire semester—meaning, for dozens of hours of teaching—in a minute or less.

But I never counsel students against using notes, and I highly recommend solid sermon preparation. Why wouldn't I? And sometimes, in major debates where every segment is closely timed, I'll write out every word of my opening statement.

I'm totally comfortable standing up to speak at a massive conference with no notes and no idea which way the Lord wants me to go until the very last second (literally). And I'm totally comfortable sending in a PowerPoint presentation of my message one month in advance if it's requested. The Lord can move both ways, and again, the way we're wired and gifted plays a big role in this too.

During the great revivals that marked the early ministry of Charles Finney, he would often speak without any preparation, just bringing the message the Lord brought to his heart when it was time to preach. But he lived in the Word, and the Scriptures constantly filled his heart and mind. Plus, he was a lawyer who engaged in very careful, systematic thought. During this season of his life, preaching without specific sermon preparation worked well.[6] But again, it's because he was immersed in the Word and was gifted with a systematic mind. That's quite the contrast from some of our rambling sermons today that are based on saying whatever comes to mind—or on really bad scholarship.

Here's a classic example that we've all heard: The Greek word for *power* is *dunamis*, from which we get the word *dynamite.* Consequently, we are told, the Spirit is the "dynamite power of God."

This, of course, is preposterous for a few reasons. First, the fact that a word in one language comes to mean something else in another language many centuries later does not affect the original meaning of the word. For example, our English word "nice" comes from Latin and French, where it originally meant "simple" and "ignorant."[7] To call someone "nice" was to call him an idiot. Does that mean, then, that we can take today's positive meaning of "nice" and put it back on Latin or French texts from a thousand years ago, changing an insult into a compliment? Obviously not.

In the same way let's just say that a thousand years from now and in a totally different language, the English word "chair" came to mean "bird." Does that have anything to do with the meaning of the word "chair" today? Of course not. It's the same with connecting *dunamis* to dynamite. We can see how the English word comes from the Greek, which speaks of power. But we can't use the word English word "dynamite" to tell us what the Greek word *dunamis* meant two thousand years ago. I hope this is clear to you.

Second, when *dunamis* went out from Jesus and into the sick and oppressed, they were healed and set free, not blown to bits (Luke 6:17–19). For example, when the woman with the long-standing bleeding issue touched the fringe of Jesus's garment, He immediately knew that *dunamis* had gone out of him—*not* because she was blown to pieces by the "dynamite power of God" but because He sensed healing power go out from Him (Luke 8:46). In the same way, when the *dunamis* of the Spirit came upon the believers at Pentecost (Luke 24:49 and Acts 1:8, both of which use *dunamis*), they spoke in new languages empowered by the Spirit. They did not die in a massive dynamite explosion.

But let's face it. Talking about the "dynamite power of God" sounds cool and exciting. Plus, we get to show off our knowledge of Greek too (or so we think!). This will fill the seats, as opposed to an accurate word study. That stuff doesn't seem to excite.

Of course, I have no interest in lifeless messages filled with irrelevant information or preached without any power or authority. Charles Spurgeon once said that, just like the cook in a restaurant doesn't come out and show you all the cooking utensils he used, preachers shouldn't get into details of the Hebrew or Greek. Instead, just like the server in a restaurant brings out your properly cooked and prepared meal, so the preacher or teacher should bring you the finished product.[8] But by all means, let it be properly prepared and properly cooked.

Yet there's a deeper problem we often have in our Charismatic circles. The leaders do prepare, but they prepare poorly, straying off into all kinds of doctrinal deviances rather than majoring on the majors. And sometimes we just stray into spiritual fantasy.

Spiritual Fantasy

Have you ever heard about receiving a "double portion" from the Lord, the idea being that if I have a particular spiritual gift or anointing, I can lay hands on you and impart a double portion to you? In other words, you will get twice what I have. Is this possible? Let's look first at the relevant biblical text.

The prophet Elijah is about to be taken up to heaven in a chariot of fire. Elisha, his closest disciple, stays by his master's side. He has a special request for Elijah: "Let me inherit a double portion of your spirit" (2 Kings 2:9, NIV). Elijah replied, "You have asked a difficult thing...yet if you see me when I am taken from you, it will be yours—otherwise, it will not" (2 Kings 2:10, NIV). And so

Elisha stayed with his teacher inch for inch until Elijah's famous ascent to heaven.

What exactly was Elisha asking for? Did he want *twice as much* as Elijah had? Of course not! Who would even think of asking for such a thing? No. Elisha wanted twice as much as the other disciples would receive. He wanted the inheritance of the firstborn.

According to Deuteronomy 21:15–17, if a man had two sons, instead of splitting the inheritance fifty-fifty, he had to divide it into three parts, giving two-thirds to the firstborn (the "double portion") and one-third to the second-born son. (The same Hebrew expression in Zechariah 13:8 is correctly translated "two-thirds": "'In the whole land,'" declares the LORD, "'two-thirds will be struck down and perish; yet one-third will be left in it,'" NIV.) The firstborn son received a *double share* of the inheritance. The same Hebrew expression is used in 2 Kings, Deuteronomy, and Zechariah. Most people have mistakenly believed that the double portion meant "twice as much"; it simply means "double share."

So what's the big deal? It is a matter of spiritual realism. We can't give something we don't have—naturally or spiritually. We can't impart "double anointings." If we think we can, we're dreaming. Yet on prayer line after prayer line, "double portions" are being handed out freely, indiscriminately, carelessly, haphazardly. Just come on up and get *zapped*. Then go out and zap the world! You don't even have to meet any conditions like Elisha did. When Elijah said it was a difficult thing, he obviously didn't know what we know. Imparting a double portion is so easy!

Let's use some "spiritual mathematics." I lay hands on Brother A and give him a double portion of my anointing. Now he has twice what I have. He lays hands on Brother B, who now has *four times* what I have. Brother B lays hands on Brother C (we're up to eight times my anointing now). He lays hands on Brother D (16 times and counting!), who lays hands on Brother E (32 times the power), who lays hands on Brother F (he's up to 64 times my "zapping" ability), who lays hands on Brother G (who now has 128 times my anointing), who lays hands on Brother H (256), who lays hands on Brother I (who gets 512 times what I have). Brother I now lays hands on me and—glory!—I have 1,012 times the anointing I had just a few seconds ago. And we haven't even gotten half way through the alphabet, let alone prayed for any of the women.

Just think of what the apostles could have done with a technique like this! If only Dwight L. Moody and Smith Wigglesworth had gotten wind of this.

"But," you ask, "doesn't the Bible tell us that Elisha performed twice as many miracles as Elijah did?" Yes, if you include the resurrection of the dead man who was thrown into Elisha's grave in 2 Kings 13. But Elisha never called down fire from heaven (Elijah did this three times), nor was he taken to heaven in a whirlwind, nor did he appear on the Mount of Transfiguration with Moses and Jesus, nor is he spoken of as the key, end-time prophetic figure, the forerunner of the Messiah (fulfilled at least in part by John the Baptist, the New Testament figure closest to Elijah). Elisha definitely did not have twice what his teacher had.

But there's more. If we can so easily multiply the power, why can't we heal really sick people more effectively? Why can't we bring more conviction on sinners? Why can't we liberate more captives? Why can't we do a better job of crucifying the flesh? You would think that with double and quadruple anointings (I once heard a sincere brother pray that the anointing on me would increase one hundred-fold!) we could do a better job.

Sorry, but it's not so simple. Remember the words of Peter: "what I do have I give to you" (Acts 3:6, ESV). He learned this from Jesus Himself: "Freely you have received, freely give" (Matt. 10:8). And what you haven't received, you can't give.

In 1990 I was at an airport in California, waiting for my plane home. I was fellowshipping with a brother I had met a few days before, when a deaf man came up to us, asking for a dollar donation in exchange for a sign language list. After determining that the man really was deaf, the brother suggested to me that we offer to pray for him. The deaf man accepted our offer, and right there in public, we prayed for his healing—but nothing happened. I said to my friend, "Well, since we didn't have the power (or faith) to heal him, let's give him a dollar." That was all we had! It would have been much better to have been able to say with Peter, "I don't have any money, but I do have faith for your healing." Unfortunately all we had was money. This jarred us back to reality.[9]

The Hundredfold Return

Here we get into even more spiritual delusion, telling people that if they give to our ministries, they will receive a "hundredfold return," meaning, they will get $100 back for every $1 they give. Talk about a "get rich quick" scheme!

Of course the people are not told how long this will take to happen, and they're reminded that God can give us this return in many different ways. But the tiniest dose of realism would tell us that, sooner or later, we will be beyond mega-rich. After all, if I give $1 today and one year later that $1 becomes $100, then if I sow that $100 back into the gospel, I'll eventually have $10,000. If I then sow that $10,000 back into gospel work, soon enough I'll have $1,000,000—that's one million dollars! And what happens if I give that entire one million to the work of the Lord? I'll end up with $100 million. Amazing!

Journalist Lee Grady notes that:

> Before his death in 2003, Kenneth Hagin Sr., the father of the faith movement, rebuked his own followers for

> taking prosperity teaching to a silly extreme. In his book *The Midas Touch*, he begged preachers to stop misusing Mark 10:28–30 to suggest that God promises a hundredfold return on every offering we give. Hagin wrote, "If the hundredfold return worked literally and mathematically for everyone who gave in an offering, we would have Christians walking around with not billions or trillions of dollars, but quadrillions of dollars!" Hagin taught that the hundredfold blessing refers to the rewards that come to those who leave all they have to serve God in ministry.[10]

Hagin was right, but that hasn't stopped people from guaranteeing the hundredfold blessing to this day, where our gullibility provides just the right atmosphere for spiritual delusions like this. Promise us anything, and we'll believe it. And what if we don't see any results? Tell us that something amazing has happened in the spiritual realm.

In 1989 I visited a large church in a large city in the southeastern United States. The pastor boasted that his congregation had engaged in so much dynamic spiritual warfare that the demonic prince over their city was riddled with holes. In fact, the pastor wondered how this satanic agent was even standing any longer. Yet when I rode up and down the streets of a busy part of that city I was shocked. There was a tremendous increase in worldliness and promiscuity since my last visit there ten years before. Even the pornography industry had greatly taken hold. The devil certainly wasn't aware he had been defeated.

The late David Wilkerson once related the all-too-common story of a discouraged pastor who said, "My church would stand with me for hours thundering over our city in tongues: binding strongholds, principalities and powers. We've bound the enemy from the east, west, north and south but the city only gets worse. There is no evidence of a change!"[11]

This is one reason people leave the Charismatic movement. What was taught and practiced didn't line up with reality.

The Sneaky Squid Spirit Controversy

In 2017 I had a Charismatic leader on my radio show before she spoke at a special conference hosted by my home congregation. Shortly after our conversation, a non-Charismatic pastor called the show, asking me if I believed in a "sneaky squid spirit." What, exactly, was he talking about? He said my guest taught that there was something called a "sneaky squid spirit," and he wanted to know if I agreed with her.

To be candid, I have lots of guests on my show, some of whom I agree with more than others. And even in the case of those I agree with a lot, there will be always be points where we differ. So, in principle, I would have no problem saying that I disagreed with something taught by one of my guests. But since I had no idea what this caller was speaking about, I wasn't about to throw my previous guest under the bus.

Not only so, but we know that Satan is quite sneaky, and I have no idea if a demon could appear to someone looking like a multi-tentacled squid. The Bible doesn't give us a catalog of demons and what they represent or how they appear, and there are plenty of odd-looking creatures described in the Scriptures, from four-faced angels to a seven-headed dragon.[12] So, as bizarre as this sounded to me, I would not immediately reject the concept.

Not surprisingly some non-Charismatic critics had a field day with this, devoting articles and web pages to bashing me and even making "sneaky squid spirit" T-shirts. I didn't bother to read most of the criticism, but I can tell you that some of it was just plain ugly, devoid of the spirit of Christ. Plus, the attacks made a mountain out of a molehill, since: 1) in more than four decades of ministry, I had never taught on this myself and I simply said I couldn't comment on it either way; 2) it's not my place to address every position one of my radio guests takes; and 3) as the same guest subsequently clarified on the air, her terminology was metaphorical, not literal.

On the other hand, I can certainly understand how, from the critics' perspective, talk like this sounded totally looney, worthy of mockery and scorn, another one of our doctrinal delusions and spiritual flights of fantasy. And because we've had so many flaky beliefs and weird doctrines over the years, even though these critics were wrong in the spirit of their attacks, they were not unjustified in some of their larger concerns. We Charismatics often have been way too loose with what we teach and preach. We do deserve some serious criticism.

The truth be told, in some of our circles, "doctrine" is almost a dirty word. It's not spiritual enough or edgy enough. It sounds old and traditional, part of the "dead" church that is strong on doctrine but weak on intimacy and too theological for its own good.

The reality is, if we want to soar into the heavenlies and do warfare in the spiritual realm, we need our feet planted firmly on the Word of God—and that means majoring on the majors and being sound in the fundamentals. And just because some churches are "taught to death," glorying in their theological orthodoxy while the world goes to hell around them, that doesn't mean we cannot be fervent in the fundamentals. Those fundamentals are the heart and soul of the gospel, our very life breath. As pastor Alistair Begg said, "The main things are the plain things, and the plain things are the main things."[13] Indeed!

Paul gave this strong exhortation to Timothy. We too should take it to heart: "Take heed to yourself and to the doctrine. Continue in them, for in doing this you will save both yourself and those who hear you" (1 Tim. 4:16).

Chapter Ten

To the Third Heaven and Back in a Flash

When Paul was taken up to the third heaven, the experience was so sacred he wouldn't describe it firsthand. Instead, he told the story as if he were speaking about someone else:

> I knew a man in Christ over fourteen years ago—whether in the body or out of the body I cannot tell, God knows—such a one was caught up to the third heaven. And I knew that such a man—whether in the body or out of the body I cannot tell, God knows—was caught up into paradise and heard inexpressible words not permitted for a man to say. Of such a person, I will boast. Yet of myself I will not boast, except in my weaknesses.
>
> —2 Corinthians 12:2–5

Nowadays people claim to whiz back and forth to and from the third heaven just as easily as they send a text message or place an order at a fast-food drive-through. With a snap of your fingers you're there, and a few moments later you're back. Oddly enough this experience doesn't seem to affect our modern-day travelers the way it affected Paul. He wouldn't talk about it; they share quite freely, without the slightest constraint.

In stark contrast Paul said that this man—again, speaking of himself—"was caught up into paradise and heard inexpressible words *not permitted* for a man to say." Other translations render with: "he heard things that cannot be told, which man may not utter" (ESV), and he "heard things too sacred to be put into words, things that a person is not permitted to speak" (NET Bible). How, then, do people who have allegedly gone to this same third heaven come back so chatty, lighthearted, and glib, describing everything they saw and heard in detail? How can they encounter something so sacred yet be so flippant about it? Something does not line up.

A. W. Tozer once wrote:

> There are many great lessons for us in the worship and reverence of the heavenly seraphim Isaiah described in his vision. I notice that they covered their feet and they covered their faces. Because of the presence of the Holy God, they reverently covered their faces. Reverence is a beautiful thing, and it is so rare in this terrible day in which we live.... *But a man who has passed the veil, and looked even briefly upon the holy face of Isaiah's God can never be irreverent again.* There will be a reverence in his spirit and instead of boasting, he will cover his feet modestly. Even if he's been somewhere, instead of coming home and bragging about it, chances are he'll cover his feet.[1]

After Jacob wrestled with the angel he walked with a limp (Gen. 32:22–32). After Job got a revelation of the Lord's majestic sovereignty, he was humbled to the dust, putting his hand on his mouth (Job 40:4). After Peter witnessed the miraculous catch of fish at the command of Jesus, he said to Him (in a boat, in the middle of the lake), "Depart from me, for I am a sinful man, O Lord" (Luke 5:8). After John saw Jesus in His glory and power, he fell at his feet as if dead (Rev. 1:17). Yet some of our leaders supposedly bounce in and out of God's heavenly courts as if they were poking their heads into a bar and saying hi to an old drinking buddy.

Where is the reverence and awe? Where is the evidence that they've really been in that holy place? Where is that limp, that humility, that brokenness, that fear of the Lord? The truth be told, there's more strutting than limping and more informality than holy fear, all of which makes you wonder if they're taking mental journeys more than spiritual journeys. As one of my friends asked about an openly carnal colleague, "How can he be so fleshly if he spends 30 percent of his time visiting heaven?" Something is not right.

In Hebrews 12 the author contrasts the Sinai covenant with the new covenant, writing:

> You have not come to a mountain that can be touched and that burned with fire, and to blackness and darkness and storm, and to the sound of a trumpet and to a voice speaking words, such that those who heard them begged that the word not be spoken to them anymore. For they could not endure that which was commanded: "If so much as a beast touches the mountain, it must be stoned or thrust through with a spear." So terrible was the sight that Moses said, "I am terrified and trembling."
>
> —Hebrews 12:18–21

Thank God we are not standing at the foot of Sinai with the voice of God thundering loudly, causing us to tremble with fear. Instead, we've come to the New Jerusalem, the glorious city set on high.

> But you have come to Mount Zion and to the city of the living God, the heavenly Jerusalem, and to an innumerable company of angels; to the general assembly and church of the firstborn, who are enrolled in heaven; to God, the Judge of all; and to the spirits of the righteous ones made perfect; and to Jesus, the Mediator of a new

> covenant; and to the sprinkled blood that speaks better than that of Abel.
>
> —HEBREWS 12:22–24

But that just means the stakes now are much higher. This is not time for reveling but for reverence:

> See that you do not refuse Him who is speaking. For if they did not escape when they refused Him who spoke on earth, much less shall we escape if we turn away from Him who speaks from heaven. At that time His voice shook the earth, but now He has given us a promise, saying, "Yet once more I will shake not only the earth but also heaven." And this statement, "Yet once more," signifies the removal of those things that can be shaken, things that are created, so that only those things that cannot be shaken will remain.
>
> —HEBREWS 12:25–27

And what is the offshoot of all this? How should we respond? "Therefore, since we are receiving a kingdom that cannot be moved, let us be gracious, by which we may serve God acceptably with reverence and godly fear. For our God is a consuming fire" (Heb. 12:28–29).

Remarkably the author of Hebrews closes this section by quoting the words of Moses in Deuteronomy 4:24, namely, that our "God is a consuming fire," reminding us that the God of the Old Testament is the God of the New Testament, and teaching us that our responsibilities under grace are far greater than those under the Law. To whom much is given, much is required! (See Luke 12:48.)

Listen also to Peter's words as he tells us how to live in light of the great price that has been paid for our salvation:

> And if you address as Father the One who impartially judges according to each one's work, *conduct yourselves in fear* during the time of your sojourning. For you know that you were not redeemed from your vain way of life inherited from your fathers with perishable things, like silver or gold, but with the precious blood of Christ, as of a lamb without blemish and without spot.
>
> —1 Peter 1:17–19, emphasis added

Peter is not talking about living in the servile fear of bondage, something that God's perfect love drives out. (See 1 John 4:18.) No, he's talking about living in reverential awe, recognizing that God purchased our salvation at the cost of the blood of His very own Son. That is nothing to snivel at. And this God who redeemed us is the same holy God to whom we will give account one day. Is it too much to think that those who claim to have seen Him face-to-face and to have looked into the eyes of Jesus in His heavenly glory, who claim that they were given spiritual secrets not disclosed to ordinary mortals, would have some reverential awe and would tread lightly in His presence?

In Awe in His Presence

In September 1989 I spent a few days with Leonard Ravenhill, who was then eighty-two years old, staying in his home, and praying and fellowshipping with him by the hour. (I was thirty-four at the time.) He had invited me to visit him so he could pour himself into me, sensing a like calling on my life for revival, and I was humbled beyond words. The first time we prayed together in his study, after just a few seconds in prayer I got on my face and wept. It was overwhelming to be in the presence of this godly giant (though he was weak and small in stature), and you can be sure I walked softly in his presence. But he was a man just like me, made of the same flesh and blood. What of seeing Jesus face to face? How intense would that be?

As I became close friends with Brother Len during the last five years of his life, I was always struck by how impacted he was whenever he prayed. He would get alone with the Lord at set times every day, even if you were there visiting with him, and when he came out from prayer, he would be devastated. "Mike," he would say to me with anguish in his voice, "the bride is naked and she doesn't know it!" He had such pain for the church and such love for Jesus, the heavenly Groom, that spending time with Him shook him to the core. How, then, can people be so casual and full of blabber about alleged trips to heaven itself?

I remember listening to the testimony of a famous healing evangelist to whom the Lord appeared early in his ministry. *He saw Jesus face-to-face.* He described in vivid detail what this encounter was like, and although it was now decades later when he told the story, you could still feel its power as he spoke of the Lord's indescribable beauty and glory. And what happened when Jesus left him? He crawled into another room and spent the entire day weeping in prayer and adoration. He was devastated by that holy encounter, and it changed him for the rest of his life. What else should we expect?

From 1991 to 1995 I had the privilege of preaching between forty and fifty times for pastor David Wilkerson at Times Square Church, often meeting with him briefly before or after the service, even having a meal with him on a rare occasion. He was very gracious in our interaction and quite compassionate if he saw a need, but I never felt totally at ease with this prophet of God. He always had that fire in his eyes—it felt as if he could look right through you—and if you had sin in your life, you would think he knew about it. I used to tell my friends that to fellowship with him was like fellowshipping with a razor blade.

But he too was just a man, frail and mortal like the rest of us. Yet I felt a real sobriety when sitting with him or preaching for him. How much soberer should we be in the presence of almighty God?

I'm all for leaping and dancing and shouting in God's presence. I know that the joy of the Lord is our strength and that there is fullness of joy in His presence. (See Nehemiah 8:10 and Psalm 16:11.) I'm all for exuberant worship and extravagant praise, wanting to be like David rather than Michal in 2 Samuel 6:14–23. And I still love to get behind the drums at the end of a meeting as the whole place erupts in celebration. I love the joy of the Lord!

But there's also a time for holy reverence—I doubt that Aaron was twisting and jumping and laughing when he entered the holiest place of all on the Day of Atonement—yet that quality is often lacking in our midst. And this leads to an obvious question: Why are we who experience the power of the Spirit and speak in heavenly tongues, and receive prophetic words and dreams and revelations, and who lay our hands on sick people and see them healed—why are we so often carnal and casual and complacent and compromised? Something doesn't line up. Add to this the claims of heavenly journeys and celestial encounters and we can only wonder: Are these people really meeting with God?

A friend of mine really liked the ministry of an evangelist who had a powerful healing ministry and often gave words of knowledge, so he decided to attend one of his conferences. My friend returned home with some real concerns. First, this preacher hardly used the Bible when he spoke. No need to do that when he often visited the third heaven and received fresh revelation there! Second, some of the alleged revelation didn't line up with the Word. Where, then, was he getting this information? Was it all a figment of his own imagination? It wasn't long after this that the man had a significant, ministry-altering moral failure. I was grieved for him but not surprised.

A spiritual son of mine has had many unusual spiritual experiences, including what he describes as heavenly encounters. But I've never once heard him describe these things in a casual way. How could he? He often has prophetic dreams, and one night he saw Satan in his dream, going about sowing discord. The dream shook him for several days, particularly this vision of the evil one. That makes sense to me. What does not make sense is the ease and ability with which some people allegedly enter into the most sacred space in the universe—the direct presence of God—and then return to earth so flippant about it. They'll even tell you how you can do it too!

In the 1980s, Nancy and I read a book about a young woman who lived in the 1800s and had experienced an intense vision of heaven and hell. After this experience, she so lost interest in this world that she faded from earthly life and passed away. We were stirred as we read her words, and the world to come became so much more real to us, as did the spiritual realm as a whole. There was something sacred about her descriptions of heaven and something dreadful about her descriptions of hell, and the picture she painted was so real. But why should we expect anything less? When Ezekiel describes the vision he received of the Lord, the closer he got to seeing God's face, the less able he was to describe it. To paraphrase, "It was something like the image of something that resembled something like…well, that's all I can say! When I saw it I fell on my face." (See Ezekiel 1:1–28.)

As a result of seeing this vision, during which he received a devastating commission from the Lord, Ezekiel was completely overwhelmed. He wrote: "The Spirit lifted me up and took me away, and I went in bitterness in the heat of my spirit, the hand of the Lord being strong upon me. And I came to the exiles at Tel-abib, who were dwelling by the Chebar canal, and I sat where they were dwelling. *And I sat there overwhelmed among them seven days*" (Ezek. 3:14–15, ESV, emphasis added).

Overwhelmed. Devastated. Dumbfounded. Stunned. Sitting seven days without uttering a word. Shocked by this divine encounter. Yes, all of that makes sense. Why, then, don't our modern prophets and visionaries, who allegedly encounter this same glorious God, hardly seemed awed at all? It's more like, "Was that cool or what? I'm telling you, God is one wild dude." Really?

Equally shocking is when worship leaders end a powerful worship time with some flippant remark, maybe even some mild profanity, to the delight of the crowd. After all, we're not religious, we're spiritual! We're not legalists, we're free! As David Ravenhill once said, "This idea that we can sin freely because we're not 'religious' is one of the greatest deceptions that has ever entered the church."[2] (Yes, David's father is the same Leonard Ravenhill I just mentioned. Like father, like son.)

A few years ago I wrote an article titled "Drunken Worship Leaders and Mercenary Musicians." (By "mercenary musicians" I was talking especially about people hired to play on the worship band at churches, even if they weren't saved.) I began by stating this:

> If there's anyone in the body of Christ who should be an example of purity of heart and purity of life, it is the worship leader, the man or woman who leads God's people into his holy presence. Yet it is increasingly common to hear about worship leaders getting drunk after church services and dropping f-bombs while they boast about their "liberty" in the Lord. Some churches even hire unsaved musicians to play on their worship teams because of their talent. How can this be happening in the house of the Lord?[3]

In the article I noted that one of my closest ministry colleagues had posted this on his Facebook page:

> There was a knot in the pit of my stomach this afternoon after I hung up the phone with a friend of mine who pastors a growing church in our city. He relayed to me an anguishing story of how some members from his worship team were hanging out with other worship leaders in a key local church. He reported to me that his team came back from that hang-out experience quite perplexed as the f-bombs were flying from the openly and unashamedly drunk worship leaders.[4]

Another pastor told me that he sent a number of young people from his congregation to train in a ministry school known for its worship. All of them came back to his church with a drinking problem, the result of hanging out with other "worshippers" in the ministry school. And on and on it goes.

It is sobering (no pun intended) to realize that Old Testament priests were not allowed to drink wine or strong drink before going into God's presence to minister. The exact wording was, "Drink no wine or strong drink, you or your sons with you, when you go into the tent of meeting, lest you die" (Lev. 10:9, ESV). What was behind this stern warning? We don't know for sure, but Jewish tradition suggests that Nadab and Abihu, the two older sons of Aaron, were drunk when they offered up unauthorized incense in God's presence and were consumed by His fire and died.[5] That's why a few verses later God warned Aaron's sons not to drink wine or strong drink before coming into the tent to minister. Is there a lesson here for us?

In Exodus 30 God instructed Moses to make a "sacred anointing oil" that would be used to anoint the items of the Tabernacle as well as Aaron and his sons. (See Exodus 30:23–38.) This anointing oil was so holy that it could not be poured on the body of a non-priest. In fact, the Law taught that "whoever puts any of it on an outsider shall be cut off from his people" and "whoever makes any like it to use as perfume shall be cut off from his people" (Exod. 30:33, 38, ESV). This was for the work of the Lord alone.

Let the worship leaders, singers, and band members come out of the secret place, anointed with sacred oil, leading God's people into a fresh encounter with Jesus the Lord. And let carnal performance and fleshly mixtures be gone. We cannot afford to play games with the presence of God.

This does not mean we have to be stiff and serious all the time. As I said before, there is certainly a time for joy and celebration and dancing and jumping and shouting. I personally love the old Holy Ghost, "camp meeting" environment, and I enjoy seeing God's people "cut loose." But how can the Spirit's presence be so strong in our midst while we remain so carnal? Doesn't divine fire burn up flesh? Doesn't divine nearness drive sin away? Doesn't the Spirit's conviction bring repentance?

I once attended a big conference in California where a respected prophetic leader was speaking. There was great anticipation for the night service, as there were thousands in attendance. After his message, he began to minister prophetically, calling out a number of individuals with striking accuracy and with words that dramatically touched their hearts. And he did so in the fear of the Lord, clearly dependent on the Spirit as he spoke. It was breathtaking and awe-inspiring. He then turned the mic over to the main conference leader who said, "Was that fun or what?"

Now that may have been this leader's style, and I don't believe he was an irreverent man. But I was immediately struck by his choice of words. Why would you describe that as "fun"? I'm not trying to be some old, dyed-in-the-wool, religious party-pooper, wanting everyone to be rigid and proper. Not a chance. But how about a little respect for the awesome gifts of God? When the Holy Spirit operates in power, to the glory of Jesus's name and for the good of His people, bringing tears and gasps and shouts, must we call it "fun"? "Fun" is chasing the dog around the yard; "fun" is wrestling with your grandkids; "fun" is playing a silly family game.

I seriously doubt Isaiah came out from his encounter with the Lord in Isaiah 6 and said to the first person he met, "Was that fun or what?" And I seriously doubt that Zacharias came away from his encounter with the Lord in Luke 1 and exclaimed, "Was that fun or what?" In fact, I know he didn't. He was actually struck dumb for questioning the angel of the Lord (Luke 1:20). Today, the angels are pals and we're practically texting them. (Perhaps that's the next thing on the list of Charismatic deceptions—an app to get in touch with your personal angel.)

Holy Longing

A few years ago Nancy set her heart to meet with the Lord, and for a period of months, she was able to clear her schedule and seek God. For years she had carried lots of responsibilities in our ministry school, but those were now given over to others, and our kids had long since been out of the house. Now she was able to focus on one thing only: encountering the Lord afresh.

We lived in a small, two-story rental house at that time, and the tiny downstairs living room was her holy meeting place. For hour after hour, she would weep in God's presence, on her knees or sitting down, often with the lights turned out, praying and reading the Word. And she did this day after day for a period of many months. It was like nothing I had ever seen before.

I was almost afraid to walk through the room at night if I needed to get to the kitchen. That's how holy the atmosphere was. And when we would sit together and talk, we were consumed with the gospel and the beauty of the Lord. It's as if Nancy freshly discovered His goodness every day, and she was devastated by that glorious discovery.

Some nights, I'd go upstairs to unwind and put on some sports for a few minutes. Immediately, though, I'd be struck with the thought, "How can I be watching sports when my wife is encountering God just a few feet away?" Within seconds, the TV was off and I was also on my knees, not in legalistic pressure but with holy longing. There's a reason the elders before God's throne are constantly in awe of His majesty and purity, proclaiming Him as holy as they cast their crowns at His feet. (See Revelation 4:1–11.)

Leonard Ravenhill told me that the most amazing words he ever heard from his esteemed friend A.W. Tozer were these: "There are occasions when for hours I lay prostrate before God without saying a word of prayer or a word of praise—I just gaze on Him and worship." Can we even begin to relate to this?

When our daughters were little, I was praying downstairs late one night, laying on my face as I talked to the Lord. A few days earlier, I had heard someone speak about everything he saw in the spiritual realm—angels and demons and heavenly encounters, and it's certainly possible that it was all true. On my end, though, despite having some very powerful experiences in the Lord, I had never *seen* things like that, and I was feeling deprived. (Thankfully, this is the only time I ever got in that frame of mind. I believe it can be dangerous to seek after these kinds of experiences.)

As I thought about what it would be like to see an angel or to be taken into God's heavenly courts, I opened my eyes, and…oh my! It was terrifying! My heart almost stopped beating and I absolutely froze—until I realized who it was. Our younger daughter, who at that time was a skinny little child, woke up in the middle of the night and came downstairs wearing her nightgown. When I opened my eyes, the first thing I saw was her tiny little leg and the bottom of the nightgown, but I was so shocked that initially I thought it was an angel. I immediately thought to myself with a smile, "If this is what happened to me after seeing my own child's foot and ankle, what would happen if I saw the Lord?"

I'm not saying that every encounter has to be overwhelming or that God can't just bathe us in His gentle love. But even *that* will be life-changing, increasing our sensitivity to the Spirit, deepening our solidarity with the Lord, and getting our hearts more in tune with Him so that we love what He loves and hate what He hates. Paul wrote, "Do not be deceived: 'Bad company corrupts good morals.'" (1 Cor. 15:33).[6] What, then, does good company do? Specifically what does wonderfully good, holy company do—as in divine company? Proverbs 13:20 tells us, "He who walks with wise men will be wise." What happens to the person who walks with the Lord—closely, intimately, devotedly? That person will become more and more like Him.

I do believe the Lord brings people into His very presence and gives others glimpses of heaven and hell, and when someone claims they've had such an experience, my first response is not skepticism. But it is not complete acceptance either. I listen with interest yet with caution. If the person has a solid track record in the Lord, I listen with even more interest. And if what they say is in harmony with Scripture, then I wonder, "Could this be true?" And if I can see they have been changed by this experience, and if I sense the Spirit on it, then I take it even more seriously.

But the last thing I'm going to do is believe every report of a heavenly journey or angelic visitation just because someone said it happened, especially if I don't see corresponding fruit that lines up. By all means, let's be believers, not skeptics, but let's be believers with our heads screwed on right. As Paul exhorted the Corinthians, "Brothers, do not be children in your thinking; rather be infants in evil, but in your thinking be mature" (1 Cor. 14:20). Being mature means not believing every wind of doctrine, not automatically embracing every report, not trivializing the sacred and holy.

Here too, it's time we grow up. God wants to entrust us with far more of His presence, but if we're not grounded and mature, His holy presence will burn us up rather than light us up.

Chapter Eleven

Wanting to Be Wise Like the World

It's amazing how the pendulum can swing. In the early days of the modern Pentecostal movement a lack of education was almost a virtue. As I heard more than once in the circles in which I came to faith, the Bible tells us that Peter and John were "unlearned and ignorant men" (Acts 4:13, KJV), and if it was good enough for them, it's good enough for us.[1] Today our university and seminary professors boast about their degrees from the leading liberal universities. We're just as smart as the world!

In the early days of the movement our churches were anything but sophisticated. We gloried in the fact that the Azusa Street Revival took place in a converted barn, and we joyfully pointed out that the principal leader in the outpouring, William Seymour, was a simple black man, blind in one eye. It was said that he so abhorred the spotlight that during the services he sometimes hid his head behind a shoe box lest anyone should focus on him. Today, our pastors adjust their sermons based on what's trending on Twitter, and their outfits must be cutting-edge. We are just as slick as the world!

Of course I'm all for solid education, but as a tool, not an idol or status symbol. And I'm all for doing things with excellence, but not as a replacement for the Spirit's power. Unfortunately we have fallen into the trap of trying to win the world by becoming like the world rather than trying to win the world by becoming like Jesus. And we have forgotten that the reason the Charismatic church around the globe is seeing the greatest harvest in history is not because of our education or sophistication. It is because of the power of the Spirit.

Paul asked the Galatians a piercing question, and we should ask it afresh in our Pentecostal and Charismatic churches today: "Are you so foolish? Having begun by the Spirit, are you now being perfected by the flesh?" (Gal. 3:3).

In context Paul was referring to relying on the works of the Law to be saved, as if you could be saved by grace through faith but only reach your spiritual goal by getting circumcised and observing the Torah. He made absolutely clear that this was another gospel entirely, one that was not really a gospel at all. (See Galatians 1:6–10.) But the principle remains the same: if something is birthed in the Spirit, it will not reach its goal (or attain maturity) by leaning on the flesh. As the New Living Translation paraphrases, "How foolish can you be? After starting your new lives in the Spirit, why are you now trying to become perfect by your own human effort?"

As for thinking that we can impress the world by being like the world—by proving we're just as smart and sophisticated and savvy—this really begs the question: Why would we want to impress people who don't know the Lord, especially with our own efforts? Do we want their praise? Their commendation? Their approval? Can you imagine Jesus basking in worldly praise?

Corinth and the Appeal of Worldly Wisdom

Like many others in the ancient Greek world, the Corinthians were impressed with the wisdom of the world, with the spirit of the age. They wanted to be smart and sophisticated like the great rhetoricians and philosophers. They measured people by the wisdom of this age, because of which they were in danger of missing the wisdom of God.

Paul addressed this head-on, beginning in the first chapter of his first letter to the Corinthians: "For to those who are perishing, the preaching of the cross is foolishness, but to us who are being saved it is the power of God. For it is written: 'I will destroy the wisdom of the wise, and will bring to nothing the understanding of the prudent'" (1 Cor. 1:18–19, with reference to Isaiah 29:14). So much for the wisdom of this era!

Paul then asked a series of questions designed to get the Corinthians to wake up to reality. And note that at the time Paul was writing, commentators believe there were about fifty to seventy-five believers in the city, so the "church of Corinth" was quite small, and we can assume that most (or all) of the believers knew one another. The apostle is saying, "Look around and see! You are hardly an impressive bunch." He asks:

> Where is the wise? Where is the scribe? Where is the debater of this age? Has God not made the wisdom of this world foolish? For since, in the wisdom of God, the world through its wisdom did not know God, it pleased God through the foolishness of preaching to save those who believe. For the Jews require a sign, and the Greeks seek after wisdom. But we preach Christ crucified, a stumbling block to the Jews and foolishness to the Greeks. But to those who are called, both Jews and Greeks, we preach Christ as the power of God and the wisdom of God. For the foolishness of God is wiser than men, and the weakness of God is stronger than men.
>
> —1 Corinthians 1:20–25

God is one eternal step ahead of the world, and so He uses the "foolish" message of the cross, which declares that He saves humanity through a crucified Jew, to confound the wise. So much for human boasting. So much for fleshly wisdom. So much for glorying in our intellectual prowess and our philosophical depth. The cross smashes that mind-set and obliterates all pride.

Paul continues:

> For observe your calling, brothers. Among you, not many wise men according to the flesh, not many mighty men, and not many noble men were called. But God has chosen the foolish things of the world to confound the wise. God has chosen the weak things of the world to confound the things which are mighty. And God has chosen the base things of the world and things which are despised. Yes, and He chose things which did not exist to bring to nothing things that do, so that no flesh should boast in His presence. But because of Him you are in Christ Jesus, whom God made unto us wisdom, righteousness, sanctification, and redemption. Therefore, as it is written, "Let him who boasts, boast in the Lord."
>
> —1 Corinthians 1:26–31

Interestingly Paul himself was a brilliant man and his educational background was the opposite of Peter's and John's. He studied with the greatest Jewish teacher of his day and he had plenty of formal training. But he understood that God did not save people through his wisdom, rhetoric, or learning. Quite the contrary.

Read his words here carefully. Over the years, they have challenged me many times in terms of my own ministry work. Again, the New Living Translation says it well:

> When I first came to you, dear brothers and sisters, I didn't use lofty words and impressive wisdom to tell you God's secret plan. For I decided that while I was

> with you I would forget everything except Jesus Christ, the one who was crucified. I came to you in weakness—timid and trembling. *And my message and my preaching were very plain. Rather than using clever and persuasive speeches, I relied only on the power of the Holy Spirit. I did this so you would trust not in human wisdom but in the power of God.*
>
> —1 CORINTHIANS 2:1–5, EMPHASIS ADDED

Paul is quick to say that among the mature he imparts wisdom. "But," he adds immediately, "not the kind of wisdom that belongs to this world or to the rulers of this world, who are soon forgotten" (1 Cor. 2:6, NLT). Rather, it is Jesus "in whom are hidden all the treasures of wisdom and knowledge" (Col. 2:3). When we get our eyes on methods and educational degrees, it's easy to get our eyes off Him.

My Personal Charismatic Crisis

In the church in which I was saved, we were discouraged from reading outside books the first year or two after we accepted Christ in order to focus on the Word. And that's just what I did, reading through the Bible cover to cover five times during those first two years as a believer and memorizing thousands of verses. During one six-month period, I memorized twenty verses a day—joyfully, not legalistically—and my prayer life was vibrant during this time too. I prayed at least three hours a day and spent at least one hour praying in tongues.

Once I started college, I had less time for prayer and the Word, but I became very interested in learning Hebrew, Greek, and other ancient languages. I sensed that I was called to preach not long after I got saved, but by 1977, when I graduated from college, I had a much greater interest in teaching—really, in biblical scholarship—and the fire to preach was waning. By 1982, when I was finishing up my PhD studies in Near Eastern Languages and Literatures at New York University, I could go a whole year without praying one solid hour in a day. And rather than digging into the Word for spiritual nourishment, I was studying it more theologically and linguistically. Without a doubt, I had left my first love.

But that was not all. I was somewhat ashamed of my unsophisticated Pentecostal roots. In 1977 I left the first church I had attended, and the congregation we joined was much more acceptable to me intellectually. Our pastor was into theology and encouraged my studies. We could talk about the intersection of politics and religion, and we were barely Charismatic—if at all. Not only did I hardly pray in tongues, but I read books against tongues and the gifts of the Spirit being for today. Ultimately, I saw that the anti-tongues, anti-gifts arguments were weak, but I had large questions about our movement as a whole. "Maybe the gifts are for today," I thought to myself, "but what we see on Christian TV certainly isn't the real thing."

My goal at that point in my life was to be a seminary professor, to improve translations of the Bible, and to become fluent in traditional Jewish writings. As for the dream that once burned in me to take the power of the gospel to masses—that seemed like a distant, faint, probably unreal dream. My path was set, I knew my purpose in life, and I was quite set in my ways—but God! Through the grace of God and the intercession of friends, the Spirit began to deal with me in 1982, bringing me to repentance, renewing my burden for revival, and setting me ablaze once again. And I mean ablaze! The Holy Spirit fell on me powerfully, touching many others in the church, and zeal for the Lord began to consume me again.

In the months that followed I laid my scholarly studies at the altar and put down my doctoral dissertation, seeking the Lord earnestly for His guidance. I too had wanted to be accepted by the world. I too had wanted the approval of secular academia. I too had wanted to shed the vestiges of my Pentecostal past, now identifying as a much more sophisticated believer with a sound theology and none of those embarrassing Charismatic practices.

The Lord burned up this carnal mentality in me, and after nine months He called me to change my dissertation topic (this time focusing on the Hebrew word for healing in its ancient Near Eastern context)[2] and to finish my PhD. But now it was a tool, not an idol.

Knowledge Puffs Up but Love Builds Up

I mention all that to say that I fully understand how knowledge can puff up while love builds up (1 Cor. 8:1). I understand how easy it is to glory in the wisdom of the world and to seek the praises of the world. We think we must prove ourselves to the non-believers (or perhaps to ourselves). We want to show that we're not ignorant Pentecostals like the pioneers were. We're a new generation. The reproach of our past is behind us. We're ready for the modern world.

But at what cost? At the cost of some of the very things that matter most, the things that the Lord prizes, such as radical devotion to Him, simple faith, daring obedience, and freedom in the Spirit. (Note carefully: there's a big difference between simplistic faith and simple faith.) Some of us used to jump to action when we felt prompted by God. Now everything is so calculated. What has become of our faith? Some of us used to be unashamed of the Spirit's moving—and of our responses to the Spirit. Now, we don't want to seem fanatical. After all, that would hurt our image.

Would the wealthy and well educated become members of our churches if we acted like a bunch of holy rollers?

And let's be pragmatic here. Would our Christian colleges, universities, seminaries, and Bible schools be able to function without meeting the standards of secular accreditation? We think we have no choice but to adjust our curricula accordingly and to stack our faculty with PhDs from the most respected universities. But I ask again: At what cost? At the cost of losing our spiritual distinctives? At the cost of having professors who never experienced the baptism of the Spirit and never prayed in tongues a single time in their lives? At the cost of talking about the gifts rather than demonstrating them? At the cost of being Pentecostal and Charismatic in name only? At the cost of raising up a generation that has never experienced the Spirit's fire?

I'm all for solid education but not at the expense of the Spirit. And if we can't incorporate solid study and intellectual rigor with an ongoing encounter with the Lord, then something is seriously amiss. Somehow, Paul's brilliance and learning didn't stop him from speaking in tongues a lot (he claimed to speak in tongues more than any of the Corinthians).[3] Nor did it stop him from healing the sick and driving out demons. Why, then, must we choose between having solid education or having the power of the Spirit, between earning degrees or practicing deliverance? Could it be that: 1) we study with wrong motives in order to be accepted by the world; 2) we succumb to the idolatry of knowledge; or 3) we study with liberals and non-believers who undermine our faith?

Unfortunately all three things are true so that today, many of our brightest young scholars are more familiar with secular literature than the Scriptures and more comfortable with Bible criticism than Bible faith. And what if we required that all professors at Charismatic Bible schools, universities, and seminaries prayed in tongues regularly and, at some point in their lives, led a sinner to salvation, prayed for someone to receive the Holy Spirit, and set at least one demonized person free? How many professors would we have left?

A leading pastor in Korea told me that he witnessed a disturbing trend in many of the top churches in his nation, including Baptist, Methodist, Presbyterian, and Pentecostal. As you might know, Koreans study and work very hard, and it is important to them to send their children to the very best universities. Those studying for the ministry had this same perspective, so this national leader explained to me that pastors would earn advanced degrees at famous liberal seminaries in the United States. But when they returned to Korea, they no longer preached against sin or stood strongly on the authority of Scripture.

We have done the same things in our Charismatic circles, and now we're paying the price. The very thing that made us special, that caused us to stand out, that enabled us to do the impossible, that allowed us to see the most supernatural growth in church history has been sacrificed on the altar of intellectual sophistication. What a horrific deal.

We have exchanged the sacred for the profane, the holy for the worldly, the costly for the cheap. And in the end, what have we gained? The world that we want to impress still scoffs at the message of the cross. Instead of our young people meeting with God with tears pouring down their cheeks, many have become fascinated and seduced by the spirit of the age—all because we failed to major on the majors. All because we sought to do the work of the Spirit in the power of the flesh. All because we did the opposite of what Paul counseled and preached.

My college and university studies were all at secular schools—my bachelor's, master's, and doctoral degrees—and I never once sat under a believing professor. Some were outright skeptics, quite hostile to my faith. Others were very friendly but totally liberal in their perspective. Still others were religious themselves, but not believers in Jesus. Yet this was where God called me, and it was great for me to be challenged all those years and to cut my teeth on opposing viewpoints. Still, along the way, I started to get off track—not losing my faith but losing my fire—and it was only by God's gracious intervention that my fervor was restored.

Since the early 1980s I've had the joy of being a visiting or adjunct professor at seven leading seminaries, and I've taught at or led ministry schools for more than thirty-five years. I've also written technical commentaries on biblical books and engaged regularly in apologetics and debates. So yes, yes, yes, let scholarship be used as a tool. But be sure to go the way of the cross first, nailing your pride and self-dependence to that rugged tree and crucifying your desire to be somebody in the eyes of the world. And be sure to put being full of the Spirit before being full of secular knowledge. After all, from a biblical perspective, which is more important, analyzing the textual and linguistic history of a scriptural text or doing what that text says? Which is more important? Demonstrating your familiarity with Bible criticism or practicing intimacy with the Author of the Bible?

Again, it doesn't have to be either-or, but in many cases, our up-and-coming scholars end up being seduced by the wisdom of the world so that they lose the fire of the Spirit. In that case, better to skip the worldly-wise education than to lose the fire.

I personally long for the day when God will raise up an army of highly educated, deeply intellectual, and mentally sharp radicals, men and women like Blaise Pascal with minds on fire and souls aflame. It will be wonderful to hear them refute the cultists and confute the atheists, providing us with a revolutionary strategy to take this generation for Jesus and shake this society for the King. My own life has been shaped by my educational experiences, and

I would not be able to do most of the things I now do in Jewish ministry (especially apologetics) or biblical scholarship without that training. But it is only a tool, not an idol, and I willfully—and joyfully—"go to [Jesus] outside the camp, bearing the disgrace He bore. For here we do not have an enduring city, but we are looking for the city that is to come" (Heb. 13:13–14, NIV). We are only passing through.[4]

During the Brownsville Revival, I contributed an article to an honorary volume for my primary professor at New York University, Baruch Levine. Often in such collections, your academic bio is listed in the beginning or end of the book (if at all), and only your name appears with your article. But in this case, right beneath the title of your article, your academic affiliation was listed, and in this volume the list was quite impressive. There were scholars from Harvard, Yale, and Stanford universities, and then Michael L. Brown, Brownsville Revival School of Ministry. I had to eat some humble pie! The same thing happened to me with a technical, scholarly article I wrote for a major Semitics journal. None of my seminary affiliations were listed (any of them would have sounded better). Instead, I was from Brownsville Revival School of Ministry. So much for my fleshly pride.

The World in Our Worship

But it's not just in our academics that we've gone the way of the world. We've also done it in our churches. We have a "Charismatic" form of worship, which means that everything is controlled, and everything is timed, but we raise our hands when we sing and occasionally pray out loud together. So much for Holy Spirit fire. And God forbid that we had a real visitation. That would spoil our plans.

The band must be super tight. The worship leader must be super smooth. The song selection must be super slick. As for the Spirit's presence—well, who really needs it? Our show will go on just fine without it. As for the Spirit interrupting things with a prophetic word or supernatural move—well, He really doesn't have access to the mic. As for taking extra time before the Lord to wait on Him in worship and adoration—time is the one thing that we don't have on a Sunday. Everything is programmed to the minute.

I do understand that in some cases minding the clock is essential. If a congregation is large and has multiple services, the pastor doesn't have much choice but to watch the clock. If one service runs late, there could be a crisis in the parking lot, which could produce a traffic jam on the streets, which could produce chaos in the community. I've preached in plenty of such services, and I do understand the problem, which is often a good problem to have because of church growth.

And as someone with a musical background myself, who shared the outstanding musician of the year award while a senior in high school and started college as a music major, I fully appreciate the importance of getting the music right. To this day, if a drummer is playing too aggressively during worship or the bass guitar is too loud, I find it very hard to enter in. This stuff can be a distraction.

But once again, we've let the pendulum swing way too far. How much do we really seek God for His Spirit to be present in our worship, even if it's only for twenty minutes of worship in our corporate gathering? And if we don't have time to bask in His presence together or seek His face on a Sunday morning, when does it happen? Do we have other, special times set aside for that?

Our songs have catchy openings, and the band stops on a dime on that final note, and there's a terrific guitar solo at just the right moment (all of which is fine). But are we anointed in what we do? And what about the content of what we sing? If new believers learned their theology from the songs they sang in worship, how sound would they be? How deep?

When I got saved in 1971, I encountered the inexpressible and glorious joy of the Lord day and night every time I worshipped, and it was exquisite. In fact, it was so exquisite that the Lord used it one night to reveal the depth of His love to me, leading me to promise never to put a needle in my arm again. By His grace, I was set free from drug addiction that night, which was December 17, 1971. But during that amazing encounter during worship, there was just one piano player (and she wasn't playing an electric piano either) with occasional guitar accompaniment in the background. And the songs we sang were little ditties, old hymns such as "When We All Get to Heaven," "There Is Power in the Blood," and "Draw Me Nearer," each with four verses and a chorus. They were quite different from my previous favorite songs, such as Led Zeppelin's "Dazed and Confused" and Jimi Hendrix's "Purple Haze." And considering I went to rock concerts every opportunity I had (from Hendrix to Zeppelin to The Doors to Janis Joplin to The Who to the Grateful Dead), the atmosphere in this little church could not have been more different. Yet I encountered God there in incredible ways several nights a week, and as we would pray at the altar after every service while the pastor's wife played piano, that encounter would go deeper.

Soon after getting saved, I began to play drums in the church, joined by the bassist and guitar player from my band (they came to faith right before me), and so our congregation now had a band. But nothing else changed in terms of our experience or our emphasis. It was Jesus, Jesus, Jesus moving in our midst. That's what mattered to us. The music was there to enhance the words.

Years ago a Charismatic leader in England said musicians had hijacked worship, and there's a lot of truth to his observation, but not because musicians are bad. To the contrary, anointed musicians are some of the greatest gifts the Lord has given His people, and it's a shame that we don't have more outlets for the many musicians in our midst to shine for Him. I pray that God will raise up a thousand-fold increase in anointed musicians, singers, and songwriters so that a holy music movement can shake the world. Unfortunately we've put our emphasis on the music more than the message—and certainly more than on the move of the Spirit—which is why we can have great music but little anointing.

Some churches have gone so far as to introduce worldly songs to be culturally relevant. If that's the case, they might as well as read from the newspaper rather than the Bible when it's time for the message. Or maybe reading from a raunchy novel would be even better? The truth be told, some pastors watch unclean movies and then talk about them during their messages to find common ground with the non-believer. Why not just go ahead and show the filthy flick on Sunday and forgo the singing and talking? That would really draw in the crowds, especially if you don't charge. And that would certainly demonstrate that your church is not one of those legalistic, stiff, religious congregations.

"Is This the Jesus Way?"

We even think the key to church growth is found in secular business books. Surely these wealthy entrepreneurs have the key! One of my friends pastored a small congregation but was friendly with some of the most prominent pastors in his city, men with thousands in their flocks. At a breakfast gathering one morning, they were talking about the latest business books they had read as they sought to implement these plans in their church. My friend, who was a deeply spiritual man with a real love for the Lord, asked them humbly, "Is this the Jesus way? Are we looking to earthly models more than kingdom models? Do secular manuals have more wisdom than God's Word?" With a look of embarrassment, they agreed, and the subject quickly changed.

That doesn't mean we run our churches in a slipshod way. And it doesn't mean businessmen don't have great spiritual ideas. Often they do, since they think outside the box and are sometimes in better touch with the needs of the community than we are. Let us brainstorm together and let us challenge our paradigms. Count me in. And where the business world has relevant insights, great. But let us not look to worldly wisdom rather than divine wisdom, to secular models rather than scriptural models, to the flesh rather than the Spirit. The dead bones of our dying world will not live without breath from above.

Other leaders do not focus on secular business models and worldly philosophies but look instead to the pomp and ceremony of church tradition. They need titles and robes and recognition, the more exalted the better, even though this was not part of their background and even though it's in violation of their spiritual roots. It would be one thing if they were raised in a high church tradition, and clerical robes were as natural to them as jeans were to a youth pastor and special titles were just a means of identification.

God knows our hearts, and the humblest minister in the room might be the one with the longest title and most conspicuous ministerial garb. In many church circles, titles like "bishop" carry great weight in the community, and they are carried with honor by those who bear the name. And perhaps being called "apostle" is no different for you than someone else being called "pastor." Outward appearances can be deceiving. One of the saintliest men I ever met wore a clerical collar. In fact, I own a book called *Underground Church* that is a sustained critique of the "institutional church" and chock full of radical challenges. Yet it was written by an Episcopal priest (surprise!) who went by the title of "Father" and whose picture on the back looks as traditional as they come.

To be clear, then, my issue is not with robes and titles in themselves. It is with the attitude of the heart and the direction of the soul. Once we didn't need all the regalia. Once we didn't need the flowery titles. We were content to be known as Pastor or Mr. or Dr. or by our first name. We were content to wear a suit and tie or casual outfit or whatever our custom was. Now, we must be the exalted clergy, even though the New Testament knows nothing of a clergy-laity distinction and even though leaders are called to serve.[5] Now we must look like kings. How in the world did we end up here?

I seriously doubt we would have made these changes if we were in the midst of a mighty outpouring. I seriously doubt we would have gotten so caught up in outward things if we were walking with our first love. I seriously doubt we would have gone in this direction if we were getting our hands dirty in direct outreach to a lost world.

Again, I make no judgment from myself on any individual, and every case is different. I simply ask my fellow leaders to search their hearts before God. Are you replacing the Spirit's anointing with something else? Is the Father's recognition no longer enough? Must we be big shots in the eyes of man? Have we forgotten the Lord's words that the first will be last (Matt. 20:16), that whoever exalts himself will be abased (Matt. 23:12), that what is highly esteemed in the eyes of man is detestable in the eyes of God (Luke 16:15)? Are we preachers or performers, servants or superstars, evangelists or entertainers?

The Scottish evangelist James A. Stewart wrote:

> I was once told that I would never be a very popular evangelist because I did not sufficiently "sell my personality."

> Oh, the shame! Our business is to magnify the Christ of God and not to fling about our personalities. Dr. Herbert Lockyer, in pointing out the peril of man-worship in evangelism, says, "If a man is somewhat attractive, blessed with a fascinating personality and with power to influence multitudes, that man is often sought after rather than the Master."[6]

Taking this even further, Amy Carmichael, the lifelong missionary to India, penned this poignant poem titled "No Scars?"

> Hast thou no scar?
> No hidden scar on foot, or side, or hand?
> I hear thee sung as mighty in the land;
> I hear them hail thy bright, ascendant star.
> Hast thou no scar?
>
> Hast thou no wound?
> Yet I was wounded by the archers; spent,
> Leaned Me against the tree to die; and rent
> By ravening beasts that compassed Me, I swooned.
> Hast thou no wound?
>
> No wound? No scar?
> Yet, as the Master shall the servant be,
> And pierced are the feet that follow Me.
> But thine are whole; can he have followed far
> Who has no wound or scar?[7]

Stop for a moment and ask yourself, "Am I scarred?"

Perhaps the solution for all of us (and I include myself here) is to rediscover that secret place, alone with God. Perhaps we need to shut the door and get back on our knees, spending extended time in what some have referred to as "throne ministry." Perhaps if we focused more on things above, on pleasing our Father and being with Jesus, we would be much more effective here on earth. Perhaps if we were more fully clothed with the Spirit, we would not to need to clothe ourselves (indeed, cover ourselves) with academic achievements and spiritual sophistication. Perhaps we just need to slow ourselves down and sit at the Lord's feet. This might just revolutionize our lives.

Chapter Twelve
Where Do We Go From Here?

In the Book of Revelation, Jesus brought strong words to the churches of Asia Minor, rebuking five out of the seven congregations in no uncertain terms. (See Revelation 2–3.) Yet in each and every case He ended His words with hope and a promise.[1] The Lord wounds in order to heal; He smites in order to make well.[2] As Jesus said to the church in Laodicea, "Those whom I love, I rebuke and discipline. Therefore be zealous and repent" (Rev. 3:19).

If what I have written on any of these pages has stung you, thank God for His merciful correction. If any of these words have hit home, be grateful that it's not too late for change. As the legendary missionary Adoniram Judson (1788–1850) once said, "The future is as bright as the promises of God."[3] Without question those promises are bright!

Even if the Lord sees fit to humble you to the dust, it is only so that He can raise you back up—but this time, more like Jesus, more dependent on His Spirit, more true to the Word, more dead to the flesh. That is the place of exalted service!

And to all my Charismatic and Pentecostal friends who have found comfort and assurance in this book, I'm so glad that you resonated with what you read. I'm only sorry that more of us in leadership did not speak and act more clearly and decisively over the years. That would have saved so many of you from pain, embarrassment, grief, and confusion. Please forgive those of us who have been silent or indifferent or even compromised for too long. And please extend forgiveness to those who come in repentance and say, "I blew it! I was guilty of some of the abuses described in *Playing With Holy Fire*. From here on I really want to honor the Lord and serve His people."

Four Things We Must Do

So, then, where do we go from here? As the Spirit continues to move mightily around the globe, how do we strengthen our foundations, correct our errors, and move forward in faith and fire? Here are four things we can—and must—do.

1. We must pursue intimacy with the Lord and immerse ourselves in the Word.

Is there anything more foundational than fellowship with Jesus and immersion in God's Word? The more closely we walk with Him, the godlier we will be. The more deeply we are grounded in the Word, the sounder we will be. The more we major on the majors, keeping the main things central, the less we will drift off into doctrinal error, deception, and sin.

Have you heard the old saying that either prayer will keep you from sin or sin will keep you from prayer? (I've heard it applied to the Word as well. Either the Word will keep you from sin or sin will keep you from the Word.) It's true!

I personally believe it's impossible to spend *quality time* with God in prayer and the Word—I mean really meeting with Him in prayer and really digesting His Word on a regular basis—without changing for the better. Either we will harden our hearts to the Lord's leading and correction, running away from that place of intimacy, or we will turn away from sin, renounce the flesh, and surrender to our Master.

Hebrews 4:12–13 says this: "For the word of God is alive, and active, and sharper than any two-edged sword, piercing even to the division of soul and spirit, of joints and marrow, and able to judge the thoughts and intents of the heart. There is no creature that is not revealed in His sight, for all things are bare and exposed to the eyes of Him to whom we must give account."

Quality time with the Lord and His Word will expose the arm of the flesh and reveal our carnality, and we will have two choices alone: humble ourselves and repent, or harden our hearts and run. Which will it be?

I once heard about a leader who allegedly spent hours alone with the Lord every day, basking in worship music and communing with the Lord. But he was so carnal in other ways, by which I mean walking in serious sins of the flesh. Yet I was told that his wife used to complain about how much time he spent with God. How could this be?

When I talked with Nancy about it, she said, "He may be going through the motions, but there's no way he's actually meeting with the Lord in deep worship. If he was, he wouldn't be getting drunk or committing adultery."

Sometime after that I was talking with a friend of the man's wife, herself a respected woman of God who knew the couple very well. So I asked her how this man could be so intimate with the Lord, such a man of deep prayer and worship, yet living in such sin. She told me, "He wasn't praying and worshipping. He was playing video games." That makes sense!

2. We must put our emphasis on being disciples and making disciples.

I once heard the story of a public speaker who brought a giant vase onto the platform and filled it to the top with big rocks. He then asked the audience, "How many of you think the vase is full?" They all raised their hands in affirmation.

Then he brought some very small rocks and let them drop into the spaces between the big rocks until there was no more room.

Again he asked, "How many of you think the vase is full?" This time, fewer people responded, recognizing they were wrong the first time around.

He repeated the exercise with pebbles, then finally with sand, after which everyone agreed that the vase was totally full. What was the purpose of his demonstration? I thought the answer was obvious: "There's always room for more!"

I was totally wrong. The speaker's point was this: Put the big rocks in first, otherwise you won't have room for them later. What a great illustration!

This is what we need to when it comes to gospel priorities. We need to major on the majors and give our attention to what matters most. If we don't put this first, everything else will crowd what matters most.

Why are we here on this earth? To know God and to make Him known. To be disciples and make disciples. Everything else we do—in our personal lives and marriages and families and jobs and free time—is subservient to that.

We must grow in our relationship with the Lord and in the character of the Lord, meaning we must grow in the fruit of the Spirit, grow in integrity and honor, grow in maturity and discipline, grow into the image and likeness of Jesus. This is our ultimate goal, in this world and the world to come. (See Romans 8:29.) And as we do this, we must reach out and give ourselves to the Great Commission. That's why we've been anointed with the Spirit's power (Luke 24:44-49; Acts 1:8): to make the resurrected Son of God known to a lost world and to strengthen His people to do His work.

And when we make the plain things the main things, to borrow a phrase again from pastor Alistair Begg,[4] the silly stuff falls by the wayside. We're too busy walking with the Lord and laboring in the harvest fields to play foolish games. "Back to the basics!" I hear the Spirit saying.

3. We must get our own houses in order and redemptively confront those who are in error.

I know we don't want to quench the Spirit (or, worse still, speak against the Spirit), and I know we try not to be judgmental. But it's one thing to be judgmental and Spirit-quenching; it's another thing to address and confront error. Failing to do so actually quenches and grieves the Spirit. Why have we allowed so many abuses to continue in our midst? Why are we so reluctant to correct and rebuke?

It's not everyone's place to confront a sinning (or straying) leader, but surely it is the place of some of us, even to appeal to that person with a spirit of humility and grace. Why do so few of us do this?

Have we forgotten that "open rebuke is better than secret love" (Prov. 27:5)? Do we no longer believe that "faithful are the wounds of a friend, but the kisses of an enemy are deceitful" (Ps. 27:6)? If we really love people, why don't we tell them the truth? If we really reverence the Spirit, why are we so silent? If we really honor the Lord, why don't we act with more holy jealousy?

I know that those of us who used to be part of legalistic, highly judgmental churches don't want to repeat the same mistakes. And I understand that those who came up from spiritually reserved backgrounds love to bask in the liberty of the Spirit.

But I ask again: Why one extreme or the other? Why not be biblical, embracing what is good and rejecting what is wrong? Wouldn't the Spirit be poured out in our midst with much greater power if we didn't make such a mess of things? Wouldn't God use us more if we were more accountable?

It's true that in many cases most of us have no access or platform to reach out to abusive leaders, let alone correct them. But we can vote with our feet and with our finances, finding another church home where the pastors serve as true shepherds or refusing to support a ministry that propagates and practices error. If enough believers demand accountability, change will come. If enough of us grow out of our gullibility, the scams will cease to succeed.

But let me issue a word of caution here as well. Whatever we do, let's be redemptive. If a leader has sinned, let's work toward true repentance and restoration, not condemnation and rejection. Treat others the way you would want them to treat you.

4. We must have a fresh encounter with the Holy Spirit.

The great cure for complacency and compromise is a fresh visitation of God's refining fire. (See Malachi 3:1–5.) The great cure for flesh and folly is a fresh encounter with the living Lord. The great cure for professionalism and posturing is a fresh immersion in the Spirit's power. The games will stop. The showmanship will stop. The abuses will stop. The carnality will stop. Or else.

Ironically one of the greatest weaknesses in our movement today is that many are building their ministries on past experiences, on what happened years ago, or on the skills they have acquired over years of service—but often without the ongoing presence of the Holy Spirit. Others are simply building their ministries on fleshly charisma and power, substituting what the flesh can do for what the Spirit can do. So we are Pentecostal and Charismatic in name only.

That means that, contrary to what our critics say, the problem is not that we put too much emphasis on the Spirit. The problem is that we do not have a deep enough encounter with the Spirit. Having Him at work mightily in our midst will bring streams of refreshing to the weary, deep repentance to the worldly, and powerful rebuke to the wayward. That which is built on flesh will be exposed; that which is built on (and by) the Spirit will survive the fire. In fact, it will come out shining more brightly than ever before.

What, then, will it be? Will we continue to play with holy fire, or will we be purified by that sacred flame? Encountering the fire of God afresh—the refiner's fire; the consuming fire; the baptism in the Spirit and fire—will change us forever and will glorify His name.

And so we pray, "Lord, send the fire! We want to become holy torches for You."[5] And let all God's people say, "Amen!"

Postscript
A Loving Word to the Charismatic Critics

In the preface I stated that I was not writing this book *for* the critics but rather *despite* the critics, since my desire was not to please or impress them, and I was fully aware that much of the contents of this book would only add fuel to their fire. But if you are a critic of the modern Charismatic movement and you are reading this book, then allow me to speak to you directly. You see, in some ways this book is an apologetic *for* the Charismatic church rather than *against* it.

How so, you wonder? (Or perhaps your thoughts are much stronger, such as, "Are you crazy? This book proves the Charismatic movement is not of God!") Well, common sense would tell you that if I shared your passion for the Word, your concerns about spiritual abuses, and your jealousy for the Lord's reputation—which I do, quite deeply—then I would have walked away from the movement years ago if it wasn't real. The fact is I've seen God do the most extraordinary things in my own life and ministry as well as in the lives and ministries of those I know and love, so I'd have to be a downright fool to deny the Lord's supernatural working.

More than that the fellowship I've had with the Lord, the outpourings of the Spirit I've experienced, and the words that He has spoken to me are as real as the air I breathe and as undeniable to me as my salvation. The serious abuses I outlined in this book (and they are just a representative sampling) melt away into obscurity in light of what I've seen the Spirit do. That's how real His work is to me. I revere the Holy Spirit, and everything He does points to the Son, to the glory of the Father. This is almighty God at work, and I bow down to that work.

If you have never tasted or seen what I'm talking about, if all you can see is the flaky and the deviant and the foolish, then I truly feel for your lack. God has so much more for you, and He wants to do so much more through you.

You might say to me, "Be honest with yourself, Mike. It would be hard for you to walk away from the movement. After all, you built your whole ministry there, and that's where your livelihood comes from. So you're just not being objective."

I appreciate that thought, but it's not true. First, I could give myself full-time to Jewish outreach, where many of my ministry colleagues are non-Charismatic. Or I could give myself full-time to addressing cultural issues, where again many of my ministry colleagues are non-Charismatic. Or I could accept a full-time position teaching at a seminary and doing scholarly research and writing, where, once more, many of my ministry colleagues are non-Charismatic. So I would have more than enough opportunities to stay busy in ministry and make a living to support my family without any Charismatic connections at all.

Second, and more importantly, on several occasions over the years, I've lost everything I had in ministry rather than compromise my convictions. If I feel something is wrong or that I cannot give myself to it with a clean conscience, I'll lose the income, the influence, and the popularity in a heartbeat. God and those closest to me are my witnesses.

Third, and most importantly, I *did* try to walk away from the Charismatic movement in the late seventies and early eighties, as I mentioned earlier in the book. I bought and read books *against* tongues and healings and the gifts of the Spirit being for today.

I sat and listened to leaders who did not believe in these things. I *wanted* to separate myself from Pentecostalism, which embarrassed me at that time. But I couldn't do so without sinning against God. The testimony of the Scriptures was just too clear for me to deny and the arguments against the gifts too weak to embrace. Plus, whenever I spent quality time with God, I would sense His Spirit welling up within me, leading me to pray in tongues, and I knew this was from the Lord.

Even with all that, once the Holy Spirit dramatically revived me in 1982, I changed the topic of my doctoral dissertation to focus on the Hebrew word for healing because I had so many questions about it. I wanted to understand the subject as best as I could, using the finest biblical and linguistic resources available. And the more I studied, the clearer the Word became to me: divine healing is for today.

That's why, even if I never saw a single person healed, I would still believe healing was for today. *My faith is not based on experience but on the Word.* I walk by faith, not by sight. The positive experiences I have had in the Holy Spirit confirm what is written rather than dictate my theology. It's the Word first, confirming experience second.

Ironically, many cessationists accuse us Charismatics of basing our faith on experience rather than Scripture, but I've often found the reverse is true. That is to say, the primary reason I believe the gifts of the Spirit are for today is the testimony of Scripture, which is then secondarily confirmed by experience. In contrast, the primary reason many cessationists don't believe in the gifts—at least from what I've heard from many of them over the years—is experience. They say, "Well, I used to be Pentecostal, but I saw so many flaky things happen." Or, "Yes, I tried that Charismatic stuff, but it didn't work. Friends prophesied that my uncle would be healed and he died." Or, "Just look at those loonies on Christian TV. Only a fool would believe their claims."

Well, you might have had terrible experiences, you might have received false prophecies, and there may be some loonies on Christian TV. But what does the Word say about healing and miracles and prophecies and tongues? That's what ultimately matters.

That's why, in my book *Authentic Fire: A Response to John MacArthur's Strange Fire*, I have a long chapter titled "*Sola Scriptura* and Therefore Charismatic."[1] And that's why, after the book came out, I began to hear from cessationists who confessed to me, "It's true. I used to be Charismatic but had some bad experiences, and I left the Charismatic church. But when I read your book, I was convicted by the testimony of Scripture that the gifts are for today, so I'm trying to incorporate this into my life now."

I can say without equivocation or hesitation that I can give you a plethora of scriptures stating clearly that the gifts of the Spirit will continue in operation until Jesus returns, whereas you cannot give me a single clear verse that says they will stop before then. That, my friend, is where your battle lies, and all the flaky Charismatic preachers in the world do not negate one syllable of the testimony of the Word. And that Word says to you afresh: Don't put out the Spirit's fire! (See 1 Thessalonians 5:19.)

I wish you could get to know some of the incredible Charismatic believers I have worked with around the world, people of wonderful dedication, soundness, and integrity. I wish you could experience some of the moves of the Spirit I've been privileged to experience. I wish you could taste and see for yourself what He is doing all over the globe. If you could, while also armed with the unshakable truths of God's Word, you would never be the same. How brightly you would burn in Him! And how powerfully you would touch so many lives for His glory.

That's why I can write an entire book addressing serious abuses and concerns in the Charismatic movement and at the end of the book, my faith is stronger and my resolve deeper to experience an even greater outpouring of God's Spirit in the days ahead. As we live in these last days of great deception and apostasy, let's also realize that these last days are marked by great outpouring and harvest. As Peter said clearly, based on the words of Joel:

> "In the last days it shall be," says God, "that I will pour out My Spirit on all flesh; your sons and your daughters shall prophesy, your young men shall see visions, and your old men shall dream dreams. Even on My menservants and maidservants I will pour out My Spirit in those days; and they shall prophesy. And I will show wonders in heaven above and signs on the earth below: blood, and fire, and vapor of smoke. The sun shall be turned into darkness, and the moon into blood, before that great and glorious day of the Lord comes. And whoever calls on the name of the Lord shall be saved."
>
> —Acts 2:17–21

Don't miss out on this great, last days outpouring. Don't miss the holy, glorious forest because of some very bad trees. Dive back into the Word afresh, seek the face of God earnestly, and embrace everything the Spirit is doing today. Then let's join together to take the gospel to the ends of the earth and see the Great Commission fulfilled in our lifetimes. Perhaps you need us as much as we need you.

Notes

Preface

1. Michael L. Brown, *Hyper-Grace: Exposing the Dangers of the Modern Grace Message* (Lake Mary, FL: Charisma House, 2014).

Chapter 1: The Spirit Is Moving Mightily!

1. Robert Friedman, ed., *The Life Millennium: The 100 Most Important Events and People of the Past 1,000 Years* (New York: Life Books, 1998).

2. Since there are at least 500 million Charismatics and Pentecostals in the world today, it is no exaggeration to say that Azusa Street has impacted upwards of one billion people. See "Global Christianity—A Report on the Size and Distribution of the World's Christian Population," Pew Research Center, December 19, 2011, accessed October 19, 2017, http://www.pewforum.org/2011/12/19/global-christianity-movements-and-denominations/.

3. K. Connie Kang, "Pentecostal Memorial Is Poised for a Revival," *Los Angeles Times*, February 6, 2006, accessed October 19, 2017, http://articles.latimes.com/2006/feb/06/local/me-pentecost6.

4. *The Life Millennium*, 58–59.

5. Allan Heaton Anderson, *To the Ends of the Earth: Pentecostalism and the Transformation of World Christianity* (Oxford/New York: Oxford University Press, 2013), https://tinyurl.com/ybq5jvfs.

6. Anderson, *To the Ends of the Earth*, xiv.

7. Anderson, *To the Ends of the Earth*, 1.

8. Anderson, *To the Ends of the Earth*, 2–3.

9. As quoted in Michael L. Brown, *A Time for Holy Fire: Preparing the Way for Divine Visitation* (Concord, NC: EqualTime Books, 2008), 56; originally published as *From Holy Laughter to Holy Fire: America on the Edge of Revival* (Shippensburg, PA: Destiny Image, 1995).

10. *Los Angeles Times*, "Rolling on Floor in Smale's Church," July 14, 1906, as quoted in Tim Welch, *Joseph Smale: God's "Moses" for Pentecostalism* (Eugene, OR: Wipf and Stock, 2013), 149.

11. As quoted in Brown, *A Time for Holy Fire*, 148.

12. As documented in Michael L. Brown, *The Revival Answer Book: Rightly Discerning the Contemporary Revival Movements* (Ventura, CA: Renew, 2001).

13. Anderson, *To the Ends of the Earth*, 248.

Chapter 2: Why Are We So Gullible?

1. All emphasis is in the original.

2. All emphasis is in the original.

3. Christopher Maag, "Scam Everlasting: After 25 Years, Debunked Faith Healer Still Preaching Debt Relief Scam," *Business Insider*, September 22, 2011, http://www.businessinsider.com/scam-everlasting-after-25-years-debunked-faith-healer-still-preaching-debt-relief-scam-2011-9.

4. See, conveniently, "36 Questions About the Holocaust," question 5, Museum of Tolerance Online Multimedia Center, accessed December 20, 2017, http://motlc.wiesenthal.com/site/pp.asp?c=gvKVLcMVIuG&b=394663#2. For a definitive study, see Raul Hilberg, *The Destruction of European Jews* (New York: Holmes & Meier, 1985).

5. For other examples, see chapter 6.

6. See "1930's–1940's," SmithWigglesworth.com, accessed December 22, 2017, http://www.smithwigglesworth.com/life/193040.htm.

7. That's why Wigglesworth was known as "the man of one book." For more on this, see George Stormont, *Smith Wigglesworth: A Man Who Walked With God* (repr. Tulsa, OK: Harrison House, 2009).

8. See Gordon Lindsay, *John G. Lake: Apostle to Africa* (repr.; n.p.: Revival Library, 2014); Roberts Liardon, compiler, *John G. Lake: The Complete Collection of His Life Teachings* (Tulsa, OK: Allbury Publishing, 1999).

9. Jennifer LeClaire, "'Prophet' Insists He Was Framed for Selling Photos From His Trip to Heaven," Charisma News, April 29, 2016, http://www.charismanews.com/opinion/watchman-on-the-wall/56830

-prophet-insists-he-was-framed-for-selling-photos-from-his-trip-to-heaven.

10. Kara O'Neill, "Self-Proclaimed Prophet Claims This Video PROVES He Can Walk on Air—What Do You Think?," *Daily Mirror*, October 2, 2015, http://www.mirror.co.uk/news/weird-news/self-proclaimed-prophet-claims-video-6558600.

11. Jennifer LeClaire, "Blasphemous 'Stoner Jesus' Group Takes Bible Study to Pot," Charisma News, December 11, 2015, http://www.charismanews.com/opinion/watchman-on-the-wall/53761-blasphemous-stoner-jesus-group-takes-bible-study-to-po.

12. Jennifer LeClaire, "You Won't Believe the Pitch I Got From One False Prophet," Charisma News, July 5, 2016, http://www.charismanews.com/opinion/watchman-on-the-wall/58191-you-won-t-believe-the-pitch-i-got-from-one-false-prophet.

13. Jennifer LeClaire, "Washington Busts 'False Prophet' in Pay-for-Prayer Scam," Charisma News, March 21, 2016, http://www.charismanews.com/opinion/watchman-on-the-wall/55956-feds-bust-false-prophet-in-pay-for-prayer-scam.

14. Jennifer LeClaire, "False Prophet Makes Ill Victims Drink Disinfectant for Miracle Healing," Charisma News, December 16, 2016, http://www.charismanews.com/opinion/watchman-on-the-wall/61887-false-prophet-makes-ill-victims-drink-disinfectant-for-miracle-healing.

Chapter 3: Mercenary Prophets

1. Michael L. Brown, "Jeremiah," in Tremper Longman III and David E. Garland, eds., *The Expositor's Bible Commentary Revised Edition: Jeremiah–Ezekiel* (Grand Rapids, MI: Zondervan, 2010), 151.

2. For more on this concern, see chapter 4.

3. Lee Grady, *The Holy Spirit Is Not for Sale* (Grand Rapids, MI: Chosen Books, 2010), 105.

Chapter 4: Superstar Leaders

1. Stephen Galloway and Ashley Cullins, "Johnny Depp: A Star in Crisis and the Insane Story of His 'Missing' Millions," *Hollywood Reporter*, May 10, 2017, http://www.hollywoodreporter.com/features/johnny-depp-a-star-crisis-insane-story-his-missing-millions-1001513.

2. Love-N-Care Ministries International, http://lncministries.org/pastor.php.

3. As quoted in Smith Wigglesworth, *The Anointing of His Spirit* (Ventura, CA: Regal Books, 1994), 215.

4. "Didache," Early Christian Writings, accessed December 21, 2017, http://www.earlychristianwritings.com/text/didache-roberts.html.

5. "Didache," Early Christian Writings.

6. Lee Grady, "6 Signs of a Toxic 'Apostle'," *Charisma Magazine*, March 22, 2017, http://www.charismamag.com/blogs/fire-in-my-bones/32235-6-signs-of-a-toxic-apostle.

7. Lee Grady, "6 Signs of a Toxic 'Apostle'."

8. Lee Grady, "6 Signs of a Toxic 'Apostle'."

9. Lee Grady, "6 Signs of a Toxic 'Apostle'."

10. "Our Founders," The Voice of the Martyrs, accessed January 12, 2018, https://www.persecution.com/founders/.

11. This is the author's recollection of the conversation.

Chapter 5: Abusive Leadership

1. "Jim Jones: American Cult Leader," *Encyclopaedia Britannica*, accessed December 21, 2017, https://www.britannica.com/biography/Jim-Jones.

2. A. J. Delgado, "The Unburied Truth About Jim Jones," *National Review*, May 6, 2014, http://www.nationalreview.com/article/377369/unburied-truth-about-jim-jones-j-delgado.

3. George Vecsey, "Parent Church Is Chagrined by Evolution of Jones's Cult," *New York Times*, November 29, 1978, http://www.nytimes.com/1978/11/29/archives/parent-church-is-chagrined-by-evolution-of-joness-cult-may-be.html.

4. Bill Muehlenberg, "On Not Suffering Fools Gladly," CultureWatch, June 23, 2017, https://billmuehlenberg.com/2017/06/23/not-suffering-fools-gladly/.

5. Linda L. Belleville, *2 Corinthians* (Downers Grove, IL: InterVarsity Press, 1996), 287.

6. Muehlenberg, "On Not Suffering Fools Gladly."

7. For the definitive Dowie biography, see Gordon Lindsay, *John Alexander Dowie: A Life Story of Trials, Tragedies and Triumphs* (Dallas, TX: Christ for the Nations, 1980).

8. John Alexander Dowie, *Leaves of Healing*, vol. 15 (Zion, IL: Zion Printing and Publishing House, 1904), 718; see also "John Alexander Dowie and the Christian Apostolic Church," The Internet Archive, accessed December 21, 2017, https://archive.org/stream/johnalexanderdow00harluoft/johnalexanderdow00harluoft_djvu.txt.

9. "John Alexander Dowie," Wikipedia, accessed December 21, 2017, https://en.wikipedia.org/wiki/John_Alexander_Dowie#/media/File:John_Alexander_Dowie_in_his_robes_as_Elijah_the_Restorer.jpg.

10. Dowie, *Leaves of Healing*, 718.

11. For hundreds of years the English-speaking church has wrongly called the letter of Jacob the letter of James, as James in Greek is actually Jacob. I believe it is high time to correct this error and attribute this epistle to the apostle Jacob instead of the apostle James. For more information on how Jacob became James, see Michael L. Brown, "Recovering the Lost Letter of Jacob," Charisma News, March 11, 2013, https://www.charismanews.com/opinion/38591-recovering-the-lost-letter-of-jacob. Note also that Jude is really Judah.

12. See especially 2 Samuel 24:1–22 and 26:1–25.

Chapter 6: Unaccountable Prophecy

1. Some point to 1 Corinthians 14:3 as proof that all prophecies are to be positive in nature, but that would be a misuse and misinterpretation of the text. First, the words of Jesus, speaking prophetically by the Spirit in Revelation 2–3, are filled with rebuke and warning, some of it quite severe. Second, even within 1 Corinthians 14 Paul writes, "But

if all prophesy and there comes in one who does not believe or one unlearned, he is convinced by all and judged by all. Thus the secrets of his heart are revealed. And so falling down on his face, he will worship God and report that God is truly among you" (1 Cor. 14:24–25). Third, 1 Corinthians 14:3 is not saying that all prophecies must be "positive" (let alone designed to make people happy!). Rather, "he who prophesies speaks to men for their edification and exhortation and comfort," and this could easily include words of correction, which when properly received will bring edification and comfort. Note also that the Greek word translated "exhortation," while having elements of encouragement, can certainly include rebuke or correction as needed.

2. See further Michael L. Brown, *Authentic Fire: A Response to John MacArthur's Strange Fire* (Lake Mary, FL: Excel Publishers, 2013).

Chapter 7: Sexual Immorality

1. See, for example, Jeremiah 2 and Ezekiel 16.
2. See 1 Corinthians 6:9–10; Galatians 5:19–21; and Colossians 3:5.
3. The only details we have are in 1 Corinthians 5.
4. God is a redeemer, and there is no reason this man cannot be used by God. He is certainly not disqualified because of the sins of his biological mother and father.
5. Sinclair Lewis wrote the book *Elmer Gantry* in 1926; it became a movie featuring Burt Lancaster in 1960.
6. For a classic example, see Numbers 25.
7. This account is included in my book *A Time for Holy Fire*, 183–185.
8. Some would use Romans 11:29, speaking first about the people of Israel, to support this point.

Chapter 8: The Pep-Talk, Prosperity Gospel

1. See Terri Whitaker, *Yesupadam: Reaching India's "Untouched"* (Washington, DC; Believe Books, 2014); David H. Jinno, *Jesus' Foot: A Testimony of God's Work In and Through the Life of P. Yesupadam and the Body of Christ in India and Around the World* (Chicago: Companion Press, 2000); "How LNC Began," Love-N-Care Ministries

International, accessed December 22, 2017, http://www.lncministries.org/about-us-how-lnc-ministries-began.php.

2. Michael L. Brown, *How Saved Are We?* (Shippensburg, PA: Destiny Image, 1990), 63–65, emphasis in the original. Used with permission.

3. These five signs are drawn from my article "5 Signs of Ear-Tickling Preachers," Charisma News, June 9, 2014, https://www.charismanews.com/opinion/in-the-line-of-fire/44176-5-signs-of-ear-tickling-preachers.

4. Leonard Ravenhill, in communication with the author.

Chapter 9: Celebrating Doctrinal Deviance

1. For the record, the Greek verb for *groan* that I mentioned also occurs in Mark 7:34; 2 Corinthians 5:2, 4; Hebrews 13:17; and James 5:9, as well as twenty-seven more times in the Septuagint, for a total of thirty-three occurrences of the verb. So again, there's nothing rare or unusual here.

2. I address this in my book *Authentic Fire: A Response to John MacArthur's Strange Fire*, in a long chapter titled "Sola Scriptura and Therefore Charismatic."

3. For the opposite tendency in our midst in recent years, see chapter 11, "Wanting to Be Wise Like the World."

4. See Exodus 14:16–30; Joshua 3; 1 Kings 18:20–40; 2 Kings 6:1–7; Matthew 14:22–33; and Acts 14:8–10.

5. See Brown, *Authentic Fire*, 249–269. William P. Farley, "Charles Finney: The Controversial Evangelist," Assemblies of God, accessed December 21, 2017, http://enrichmentjournal.ag.org/200601/200601_118_finney.cfm; J. Gilchrist Lawson, "Charles G. Finney: A Brief Biography," The Gospel Truth, accessed December 21, 2017, https://www.gospeltruth.net/lawsonbio.htm.

6. "Origin and Etymology of Nice," Merriam-Webster.com, accessed December 21, 2017, https://www.merriam-webster.com/dictionary/nice.

7. This is found in Charles H. Spurgeon, *Lectures to My Students* (repr., Peabody, MA: Hendrickson, 2010).

8. Adapted from Brown, *A Time for Holy Fire,* 171–173.

9. Lee Grady, "6 Really Bad Charismatic Doctrines We Should Retire," CharismaNews.com, May 7, 2014, accessed December 22, 2017, https://www.charismamag.com/blogs/fire-in-my-bones/20325-6-really-bad-charismatic-doctrines-we-should-retire.

10. David Wilkerson, "Your Faith Is Going Into the Fire," World Challenge Inc., February 5, 1990, https://worldchallenge.org/newsletter/1990/your-faith-is-going-into-the-fire.

11. See Ezekiel 10:14 and Revelation 13:1.

12. Alistair Begg, "The Main Things," Truth for Life, September 9, 2015, http://blog.truthforlife.org/the-main-things.

Chapter 10: To the Third Heaven and Back in a Flash

1. A. W. Tozer, *Tozer Speaks: 128 Compelling and Authoritative Teachings of A. W. Tozer,* vol. 1 (Camp Hill, PA: WingSpread Publishers, 2010), chapter 17, emphasis added.

2. David Ravenhill in communication with the author.

3. Michael Brown, "Drunken Worship Leaders and Mercenary Musicians," Charisma News, February 11, 2013, https://www.charismanews.com/opinion/38195-drunken-worship-leaders-and-mercenary-musicians.

4. Brown, "Drunken Worship Leaders and Mercenary Musicians."

5. See Leviticus 10:1–2, but read Leviticus 9:23–24 first. Aaron's sacrifices offered in obedience were consumed by God's fire; Aaron's sons, acting in disobedience, were also consumed by God's fire.

6. Paul is quoting the words of a popular proverb that apparently traced back to the Greek comic Menander.

Chapter 11: Wanting to Be Wise Like the World

1. Note how the words *ignorant* and *unlearned* are rendered in other modern translations: "uneducated and untrained" (NKJV and NASB); "uneducated and ordinary men" (NET Bible); "ordinary men with no special training in the Scriptures" (NLT).

2. For my final work on this (along with a full, academic study of divine healing), see Michael L. Brown, *Israel's Divine Healer: Studies in Old Testament Biblical Theology* (Grand Rapids, MI: Zondervan, 1995).

3. In 1 Corinthians 14:18 Paul wrote, "I thank God that I speak in tongues more than all of you" (ESV).

4. The last paragraph is taken from Michael L. Brown, *Revolution!: The Call to Holy War* (Ventura, CA: Renew, 2000), 142–143.

5. See Michael L. Brown, *Revolution in the Church: Challenging the Religious System With a Call for Radical Change* (Grand Rapids, MI: Chosen Books, 2013).

6. James A. Stewart, *Evangelism*, fourth edition (Asheville, NC: Revival Literature, n.d.).

7. "No Scars?" by Amy Carmichael, © 1999 The Dohnavur Fellowship. Used by permission of CLC Publications. May not be further reproduced. All rights reserved. Published in *Mountain Breezes: The Collected Poems of Amy Carmichael* (Fort Washington, PA: CLC Publications, 1999).

Chapter 12:
Where Do We Go From Here?

1. See Revelation 2:7, 11, 17, 26–27; 3:5, 12, 20.

2. See Job 5:18; Isaiah 19:22; 30:26.

3. This is Adoniram Judson's most famous quote. For background see http://dozierdon.blogspot.com/2010/06/future-is-as-bright-as-promises-of-god.html.

4. Alistair Begg, "The Main Things," Truth for Life, September 9, 2015, http://blog.truthforlife.org/the-main-things.

5. Note that in John 5:35 Jesus said of John the Immerser, "He was a burning and a shining lamp." In another context the Word says God "makes His angels as winds, His ministers a flaming fire" (Ps. 104:4).

Postscript:
A Loving Word to the Charismatic Critics

1. Brown, *Authentic Fire*, 161–222.